Sister "Rosa Bal[illegible]
May God bles[illegible]
Benjamin Robertson
10-6-00

Led by the Spirit of God

Also by
Benjamin W. Robertson Sr.

Just As He Promised (1998)

Led by the Spirit of God

Essays and Sermons by Spirit-Filled Preachers

Benjamin W. Robertson Sr.

Providence House Publishers
Franklin, Tennessee

Printed in the United States of America

04 03 02 01 00 1 2 3 4 5

Library of Congress Catalog Card Number: 00-104914

ISBN: 1-57736-199-7

Cover design by Gary Bozeman

Scripture quotations are taken from the Holy Bible, Authorized King James Version, The Living Bible, the Holy Bible, New International Version, Phillips Modern English Version, or Williams Complete Bible Commentary.

PROVIDENCE HOUSE PUBLISHERS
238 Seaboard Lane • Franklin, Tennessee 37067
800-321-5692
www.providencehouse.com

This book is dedicated to Sugar, my wife of more than forty-five years, and our only child, Benjamin Jr., who serves as one of those in a crowd of heavenly witnesses;

to the officers and members of the First Union Baptist Church of South Richmond, the Piney Grove Baptist Church of Virginia Beach, and the Cedar Street Baptist Church of God of Richmond, for permitting me to serve them for fifty years;

to the seminarians who gave me the opportunity to help a few preachers to strive to reach their ever-receding goals;

and above all, the persons of the Godhead who have led Sugar and me all the way.

Contents

Foreword

Hon. Rosemary R. Harris

ON DECEMBER 29, 1956, THE REVEREND DR. BENJAMIN W. Robertson Sr. performed the wedding ceremony of my parents, James E. Harris Jr. and Mary Louise McPherson. This marriage represented the union of two of the oldest member families of Cedar Street Baptist Church. My father is able to trace back his family tree several generations, and my mother's lineage dates back to one of the first pastors of Cedar Street, the Reverend Jacob Turner, who served as Pastor from 1886 to 1897. This union was also significant since my parents were instrumental in Dr. Robertson being named Pastor of Cedar Street in 1955. As detailed in Dr. Robertson's book, *Just As He Promised*, I can just imagine my father canvassing door-to-door promoting his candidate in his congenial, but matter-of-fact way; and I can envision my mother in her bold, yet eloquent way, making the motion to reopen the slate to include the name of Benjamin William Robertson.

I can only imagine these events, as I was not born until 1958, with my younger brother, James III, arriving in 1961. Dr. Robertson dedicated us to God shortly after our respective births; later, in 1969, upon our acceptance of Jesus Christ as our

Savior, Dr. Robertson baptized us. As a child, I witnessed the loyalty and support given to Dr. Robertson by my father and my mother, in particular, who taught me to respect his position as Pastor. I remember vividly the rapport and camaraderie that existed between our families.

In 1979, while a student at Duke University in Durham, North Carolina, under the tutelage of the renowned historian, sociologist, and theologian, Dr. C. Eric Lincoln, I conducted a case study on Black preachers and churches in Virginia. In that paper, I wrote these words:

> At the helm of the Cedar Street Baptist Church is its central power figure, the handsome and well-dressed Reverend Dr. Benjamin W. Robertson Sr. He is highly respected by his members, using his personal magnetism to foster a close familial tie with the congregation. His mastery of oratorical skills is unsurpassed. With his fervent and emotional charged preaching, Robertson is able to talk to his congregation and they talk back to him—the true measure of a great preacher.

Even today, at the dawn of a new century, these words remain true for this uniquely gifted and talented preacher, teacher, pastor, and radio and television evangelist, who is still preaching the gospel and winning souls to Christ. I thank God for his impact upon and presence in my life. Upon the deaths of my mother and father in January, 1984, and in March, 1987, respectively, God gave me a special "earth angel" in the personage of Dr. Benjamin W. Robertson Sr. He has been with me every step of the way—through every trial, tribulation, test, tragedy, and triumph.

So it is indeed a privilege and honor to have been asked to pen a preface to his second project, *Led By the Spirit Of God*. His first project, *Just As He Promised* chronicled his life story and was both entertaining and historically instructive. In this work, Dr. Robertson shares more anecdotes, many humorous and

Hon. Rosemary R. Harris

entertaining, while incorporating a collection of inspirational and uplifting sermons from his ministerial compatriots. This work is reflective of Robertson's more than a half century spent in the Gospel Ministry. He is indeed a visionary and leader in his field, unhindered by the boundaries of tradition.

Through the years, I have marveled at his ability to tell a story, to manage, motivate, and influence people, and to preach the gospel. This second work *Led By the Spirit of God* demonstrates that with God "nothing shall be impossible to you" (Matthew 17:20).

—Rosemary R. Harris, Attorney-at-Law
Chief Magistrate, 13th Judicial District of Virginia
Director, M. M. Harris Scholarship Foundation

Foreword

Dr. A. Lincoln James Jr.

DR. BENJAMIN W. ROBERTSON IS ONE OF THE GREAT pastors of the twentieth century, having served in the pastorate of the Cedar Street Baptist Church of God for forty-five years. After more than fifty years in the Gospel Ministry, his influence continues to strive and grow by leaps and bounds. He stands as a "tall timber in the ecclesiastical forest" of God's outstanding leaders. Not only does he lead faithfully and preach with power, but his Television Ministry goes into the homes of thousands of believers each Sunday at 7 A.M.

Because of his interest in theological education and the training of church workers, the Lord led him to be the founder of the Richmond Virginia Seminary in 1981 and he served as president until May 31, 2000.

You will find it very uplifting as you read this book, *Led By the Spirit of God*. This is an exciting compilation of sermons by some of the greatest preachers of the Christian Church. The homiletic and devotional value of these sermons will inspire and encourage those who read them. As you read these messages, you will find them to be homiletically sound, Biblically based, exegetically efficient, and hermeneutically correct.

Dr. A. Lincoln James Jr.

Led By the Spirit of God will take its rightful place among the milestone contributions to the Christian Church, especially for the young preachers looking to follow those whose footsteps are ordered by God.

—A. Lincoln James Jr.
Pastor, Richmond Trinity Baptist Church
Vice-President, Richmond Virginia Seminary
President, Congress of National Black Churches
(Richmond Affiliate)

Preface and Acknowlegments

AFTER MY BOOK *JUST AS HE PROMISED* WAS NOMINATED by the Library of Virginia for Best Autobiography of a Virginia Author for 1998, I was encouraged to continue to put in writing some of the things that I feel may be helpful to those who are interested. I accepted the challenge from the fore-words of Dr. Robert L. Taylor and Dr. Percy High and I have picked some sermons and suggestions that I personally feel are important to readers. However, it must be understood that many times what we want to say is not perceived as we have desired.

To my many female friends who are preachers and church workers, I would like to apologize for continually referring to God in the traditionally masculine image. I have done so in the interest of simplicity rather than from any rigidly held concept regarding gender.

I have taken advantage of my many friends who have so much to offer and have included their works in this book, *Led By the Spirit of God*. My whole ministry has been successful because of the many friends whose wisdom and experience I have been able to filter into my ministerial style.

In 1996, Governor George E. Allen appointed me to the Virginia State Board of Psychology. I agree with those psychologists who make no distinction between the mind and the spirit, and therefore no distinction between the process of achieving spiritual growth and achieving mental growth. I believe that if one permits himself or herself to be led by the "Spirit of God," he or she will work under the guidance of the Holy Spirit.

Of course, I am aware that there is no one simple answer to the problems of our society. We cannot become spiritually mature overnight because the pathway of spiritual growth is a long journey and continues on with a never-ending, receding goal.

I cannot give too much credit to the officers and members of the Cedar Street Baptist Church of God and to Reverends Robert C. Kemp, Thomas Briggs, Jacob Turner, O. Paul Thompson, William Gray Sr., William Harris Sr., James H. Roots Sr., and John W. Kemp Sr. who served this pastorate with honor and dignity.

I am indebted to the Virginia Seminary and College in Lynchburg for permitting me to serve as its tenth President and to the trustees, faculty, staff and student body for working with me since 1981 when a little seminary was founded. All of us have watched it develop into the second largest Black seminary in the state of Virginia, second only to the Samuel D. Proctor School of Religion, Virginia Union University.

After serving in the Christian Ministry for more than fifty years and in the pastorate for almost the same number of years, I make no apology for my spiritual standing. I have seen God work things out many times for me and for Cedar Street.

Therefore, I would like to acknowledge the work of the Holy Spirit first of all. I do not have the time nor the funds to pay for the help that I have received from my wife, Dolores W. (Sugar) Robertson; my sister, Joyce; my administrative assistant, Barbara B. Kemp; the writers of the forewords; the persons who gave me the privilege to publish their sermons in this book (especially to Dr. E. D. McCreary Jr., my seminary teacher).

In addition, I would like to thank the Cedar Street officers and members and my ministerial friends for encouraging me that it was not wise for me to retire from the pastorate of Cedar Street but, instead, to serve on as long as the Lord would have me.

I know that I am honored to have served the Cedar Street Baptist Church of God since 1955 and the Richmond Virginia Seminary since 1981.

I am always grateful for my saintly mother and father, Anna Mary and Clarence Robertson, whose home and Christian teachings put me on the right pathway of life; to my best friend and wife, Sugar, who has been so helpful to me for almost a half century; and to our only child, Benjamin Jr., who gave Sugar and me so many happy days to remember.

Benjamin W. Robertson Sr.

"For as many as are led by the Spirit of God, they are the sons of God."
Romans 8:14

CHAPTER ONE

The Progressive Baptist Convention, Inc.

In 1961, it was not the general opinion that the founders of the Progressive Baptist Convention, Incorporated, were led by the Spirit of God to leave the National Baptist Convention, U.S.A., Inc., to form another group. Many were dissatisfied with what was happening but felt that the Bath House and other holdings of the National Baptist Convention, U.S.A., Inc., were too valuable just to walk away from and leave to those who remained with the established convention.

All of my life, I have become involved in things that must be explained in order for one to understand. In August 1961 the Cedar Street Baptist Church of God was a member of the National Baptist Convention of America in which Dr. Prince was the President. Sugar, Benjamin, and I had been to the West Coast in June and now the convention was meeting in September 1961 on the West Coast. Since we had already been out west, we decided that since the National Baptist Convention of America, the national convention with which Cedar Street was connected, was meeting on the West Coast, Sugar and I were not going to any national convention that September. It was Dr. A. W. Brown who called to ask me when

I was leaving to go to the Annual Session of the National Baptist Convention of America. When I attempted to explain to him why I was not going to my convention, he told me that the Pastor of Cedar Street should be present at one of the national conventions. Dr. Brown knew that it was too late for me to get a place to stay, therefore, he invited me to be his roommate at the National Baptist Convention, U.S.A.'s meeting in Kansas City, Missouri. I accepted his offer based on the possibility of getting a flight to Kansas City.

When the National Baptist Convention, U.S.A., Inc., met in Kansas City, I was there with the twenty-five-dollar representation fee that Dr. Brown had asked me to bring. On my arrival at the National Baptist Convention, U.S.A., Inc., I found out that there were two groups registering delegates for the same convention; there was a group of followers of Dr. J. H. Jackson and those of Dr. Gardner C. Taylor. I was puzzled as to which group I should register with. I was unaware of the deeply rooted problems of the National Baptist Convention, U.S.A., Inc.; therefore I followed the leadership of Dr. A. W. Brown and registered with the Taylor faction. The matter was taken to court. The court handed down the decision that there was only one convention, the one led by Dr. Joseph H. Jackson. Therefore, the court stated that Dr. Jackson represented the convention and that all funds collected by the followers of Dr. Gardner C. Taylor would be put in the treasury of the National Baptist Convention, U.S.A., Incorporated. By joining with the Taylor group and then having the funds given to the Jackson faction, Cedar Street became a member of both the National Baptist Convention of America and the National Baptist Convention, U.S.A., Inc. The last time that I had attended the National Baptist Convention, U.S.A., Inc., was in 1953 in Miami, Florida, when Dr. E. C. Smith, President of the Virginia Baptist State Convention, presided over the election in which Dr. J. H. Jackson was elected president. I was not aware of the fight over tenure for the presidency until Dr. Smith explained to me that it was the tenure of the presidency that was causing the confusion. I soon discovered that many of the pastors who were serving in the larger congregations had banded together to have the tenure of the presidency respected. These individuals felt that tenure was already in the constitution but had been overridden each year because of the popularity of Dr. J. H. Jackson. Many persons came to the convention just to hear his annual President's Address.

Since I had been encouraged by Dr. Brown to attend the convention and he had offered to share a room with me, I felt that I should vote with him for Dr. Gardner C. Taylor and help defeat Dr. Jackson. I was ready to cast my one vote in favor of Dr. Taylor. However, it was unfortunate for those who were against Dr. Jackson to have Dr. Jackson scheduled to preach before the election. Words cannot describe what a preacher he was. I sat there and witnessed one of the greatest preachers of our time electrify those thousands of people. When he sat down, I could not vote against a man who had preached as this man had. Even though two of my mentors, Dr. E. C. Smith and Dr. J. C. Austin, were also not in favor of Dr. J. H. Jackson remaining the President of the NBC, I had to follow the Spirit of God. I wanted nothing to do with fighting this preacher's preacher. Therefore, I did not vote at all.

After the convention was over and we had returned home, I went to the Baptist Ministers' Conference of Richmond and Vicinity. Dr. Robert L. Taylor, President of the Goodwill Baptist Convention, gave the news report that day. In his report, he mentioned that Dr. L. V. Booth was calling a meeting in Cincinnati, Ohio, at the Zion Baptist Church, November 14 and 15, 1961. Since Cedar Street had provided for my expenses to the various meetings of the Baptist Church Family, I told the conference that I was going. They asked me to bring back a report of the Cincinnati meeting.

This Cincinnati meeting drew representatives from fourteen states with a total of thirty-three delegates. The following individuals were elected:

Dr. T. M. Chambers, President
Dr. L. V. Booth, Vice President
Dr. J. Carl Mitchell, Recording Secretary
Dr. Louis Rawls, Treasurer
William T. Parker, Attorney

Others uniting were:

Dr. John F. Williams, Virginia
Rev. A. Ross Brent, New Jersey
Rev. Andrew J. Hargrett
Rev. C. B. Lavign
Dr. J. Raymond Henderson, California
Rev. K. C. Bass, Florida
Dr. Benjamin W. Robertson, Virginia
Rev. J. F. Green, Michigan
Rev. J. Barry Williams, Pennsylvania
Rev. D. C. Crosby, Michigan
Dr. C. C. Adams, Foreign Mission Bureau
Rev. W. V. Glover, Alabama

After the organizational meeting in Ohio there were two other meetings held before the First Annual Session in Philadelphia at the Shiloh Baptist Church, headed by Dr. W. H. R. Powell, Pastor, and Dr. Charles McCreary, Administrative Pastor. The first was held in January in Chicago at the Tabernacle Baptist Church, with Dr. Louis Rawls, Pastor. The next formative meeting was held in spring 1962 at the Cedar Street Baptist Church of God, in Richmond, Virginia, with Dr. Benjamin W. Robertson presiding. At the meeting in Richmond, some of the preachers who would become giants in the newly organized Progressive Baptist Convention, Inc., told those present that this was not the proper thing to do. They wanted to call off the Philadelphia meeting and return to the National Baptist Convention, U.S.A., Inc.

I have had the privilege to have been a part of three national Baptist Conventions: the National Baptist Convention, U.S.A., Inc., the National Baptist Convention of America, and the Progressive National Baptist Convention, Inc.

I was with the National Baptist Convention, U.S.A., Inc., from September 1953 to 1956. In 1956, the National Baptist Convention of America (NBC of America) met in Richmond, Virginia. Dr. Samuel M. Thompson of Greater Mount Moriah Baptist Church was the host Pastor. Since Mount Moriah Baptist Church was the only church in Richmond with membership in the NBC of America and one of few churches in Virginia connected with this convention in Virginia, I was persuaded to help entertain delegates while they were in Richmond.

In 1956, the main hotels were not available for Negroes to stay. Therefore, we had to open our own homes to give the delegates places to stay. Sugar and I were very fortunate to have had Dr. and Mrs. E. S. Branch, Pastor, Fourth Missionary Baptist Church, Houston, Texas, as our guests. Because of our friendship, Cedar Street Baptist Church of God became a member of the National Baptist Convention of America. Dr. Branch and I exchanged services in revivals for a few years.

In 1961, I became one of the founders of the Progressive National Baptist Convention, Inc., and our close relationship began to drift apart. Dr. Branch was the Executive Secretary of the Foreign Mission Board of the NBC of America for years while he served the Fourth Missionary Baptist Church, Houston, Texas, for more than sixty years.

Someone asked me which one of the conventions did I prefer. I answered this question by relating a story of a man who had been courting a girl by the name of Martha. Martha had a twin sister named Mary. He had been courting Martha for years when they fell in love and wanted to get married. He and Martha went to obtain their marriage license and told the clerk that he and Martha wanted to marry. In those days, it cost two dollars for a marriage license. When they got home, they were greatly surprised that the license had been made out for "Mary" instead of "Martha." He had already paid two dollars to get the marriage license. So he rushed back to the court with both Mary and Martha to show the clerk what a great mistake had been made. The clerk told the man that since the license had been made out in the name of Mary, it would cost him twenty-five cents more to get it changed to Martha. The man looked at Martha and then at Mary. He told the clerk that he would not pay the twenty-five cents more because he did not see a quarter's worth of difference between the two. So he married Mary. I have been in all three of the before-named national conventions and I haven't seen a quarter's worth of difference among them.

I have found out that all three are trying very hard to do good jobs. They are engaged in missionary work and I enjoy their annual sessions. However all of them have more chiefs than Indians. If you get in with the powers that be, you will get on the program each year somewhere. Usually the same persons are on the program year to year. One year, the person may be programed to preach a sermon in the parent body, the next year with the women, the next year in the night service, and the next year giving some kind of report. The programs usually consist of the same names in different places. I must confess that most of the time, these persons are good preachers, serving large congregations. Even though there is a power struggle, I recommend that all churches should be connected with one or more of these conventions because it gives the pastor an opportunity to meet other ministers. I enjoy the fellowship and I take great joy in observing the humility of these great preachers.

"But when Herod heard all this, he said, "It must be John whom I beheaded, risen from the dead."

Mark 6:16

"And through faith he continued to speak after his death."

Hebrews 11:4b

CHAPTER TWO

The Language of the Dead

There are other ways of talking than by speech. Animals cannot speak, yet many of them have developed definite manners of expression which they make use of as language. The deaf and dumb, who are devoid of formal speech, have developed certain symbols and signs which very definitely express their sentiments and serve as a dependable system of communication.

Language is the vehicle through which thoughts are conveyed whether they are spoken, written, or suggested. In any event, it is possible to make profound impressions upon others.

Sometimes language reveals itself most powerfully in the silence of human existence. Many times a profound message comes to us by watching the budding rose unfold its essential beauty as it develops amid the shrubbery around some backwoods frog pond.

The little ant in its busy process of storing for winter has spoken eloquently to some boy, some man, some girl, or some woman telling each one the value of thrift and industry. Many times this has caused that little boy to grow into promising manhood as a result of that lesson he learned from an ant.

I guess it is generally understood that we are talked to on every hand. For instance, the whistling breeze that plays hide-and-seek behind the towering tombstones out in the city of the dead, as well as the slow-moving stream that winds its way gracefully to the deep blue sea. They both speak to us in no uncertain tone.

The fact that we are talked to on every hand, prompted David to say, "The heavens declare the glory of God and the firmament shows his handiwork. Day unto day utters speech and night unto night shows knowledge" (Ps. 19:1).

In other words, each day that we face has its own language. Each day, in the silence of its passing, talks to us about the goodness and glory of God. Each day also talks about the value of taking advantage of the opportunities that come to us on the wings of that day.

A day lost can never be regained. All the gold in the world, nor the value of all the diamonds can purchase "one second" of a day. The hills, gullies, beautiful sunsets, and the rivers and rivulets, speak to us as they quietly perform their age-old duties. The sun, moon, and stars send out an endless message across the whole of creation. It is beautiful to listen to the language of the stars on a clear night when they are most eloquent. Therefore, language is not simply speech, but all of those acts which influence others, whether good or bad.

We come, now, to talk about the language of the dead. From what has already been said, we must agree that the dead can talk. It is true that the dead do not possess the power of speech, because in death, our feeble faltering tongues lie silent in the graves. But it is always, "Blessed are the dead that die in the Lord, yea, saith the spirit, for they shall rest from their labor and their works do follow them" (Rev. 13:14).

The language of the dead always originates from their works. This is a source of profound oratory. Deeds excel words in the process of conveying thought. That is why Jesus said,

"You will know them by their fruits. Are grapes gathered from thorns, or figs from thistles?" (Matt. 7:16). Usually what we do speaks so loud that people cannot hear what we say.

The language of the sainted dead is the greatest source of inspiration to the living. When they speak, creation stands at attention. Their sacred voices always ring out above the characteristic road of life and point us in the right direction.

There are plenty of people today who have been led to make the right decisions because, in a dream or vision, a sainted relative who has crossed the mystic river has talked with them. Of course, it may have been a mother or father, a sister or brother; or it could have been a grandmother, aunt, or uncle; or some Sunday school teacher or public school teacher; or that old preacher or church officer. Whoever it was, he or she showed us the right path and by walking in that path, we have become what we are today. The dead speak through the acts performed while they lived among us.

Herod's guilty conscience made him feel that he was hearing John the Baptist as Jesus' reputation was spreading. The people were saying that John the Baptist had risen from the dead and that was why he was showing such miraculous powers. Others maintained that he was Elijah, and others that he was one of the prophets from the old days come back again. But when Herod heard of all this, he said, "It must be John whom I beheaded, risen from the dead" (Mark 6:16).

You must remember John the Baptist was God's outspoken preacher. He came upon the scene bearing witness of one who comes after him but is preferred before him, for He was before John.

When the Jews sent priests and Levites from Jerusalem to ask Him "Who are you?" And he confessed that he was not the Christ. Then they asked, "Are you Elijah?" John answered, "I am the voice of one crying in the wilderness, make straight the way of the Lord." They asked him then, "Why do you baptize, if you are not that Christ?" John answered, "I baptize with water; but there stands one among you, whom you know not; it is he who comes after me, is preferred before me, whose shoe latchet I am not worthy to unloose" (Matt. 3:3).

John was so outspoken that he even questioned whether Jesus was really the Messiah or not. John had been in prison and Jesus had not been to visit him as he thought Jesus should have.

Therefore, John sent two of his disciples and said to Jesus, "Are you he that should come, or look we for another?" Jesus answered and said unto them, "Go and tell John again those things which you have heard and seen. Tell John that the blind received their sight, the lame walk, the lepers are cleansed, and the deaf can hear, the dead are raised up, and the poor have the gospel preached to them" (Luke 7:19–20).

When John the Baptist heard that King Herod had taken his brother Phillip's wife and had married her, John went to Herod. John made his never-fading speech, "It is not right for you to have this woman." Herod wanted to kill John the Baptist for this but he was afraid of the people, since they all thought John was a prophet. However, Herod was just a tool in the hands of a powerful woman, Herodias, Phillip's wife. It is said that Herod would have gladly listened to John, but he could not stand up against this powerful woman. If he had listened to God's faithful prophet and put away Herodias, he would have been greatly helped.

We must confess that without the power of God no safeguard can protect a weak man from the most absurd alarms of a strong woman. The persistence of John's message led Herod to a position in which two women, a mother and her daughter, were able to spring up and poison his enjoyment in an unexpected hour of his birthday party.

A bad woman can ruin a weak man. Herodias, the woman who was married to King Herod's brother, Phillip, quarreled against John. She wanted him killed. The only reason that she could not is because Herod feared John. He was not only afraid of the people but he knew that John was a just and holy man. Therefore, Herod refused to have John killed. Yet, Herodias turned on her charm and convinced Herod to have John arrested. Therefore, the king had John arrested and bound him in prison.

Herodias was not satisfied with John just being in prison. She still wanted him dead. She waited to find the opportunity to have John killed. So that opportunity came at the birthday supper of King Herod. King Herod wanted to have a great celebration; therefore, he invited all his lords, captains, and the very big shots of Galilee to help him celebrate his birthday by dining with him.

During the supper, Herodias's daughter (who really was the King's niece) danced before the king. She danced so well that it pleased the old man and those who sat with him. He was so amused and excited that, when she had finished dancing, Herod said to her, "You just ask me for anything you like and I will give it to you." Usually when a person has been drinking, his or her ego goes up. So he asked her again, the second time with more emphasis. He said, "I swear that whatsoever you ask of me, I will give it to you, even if you ask me for half of my kingdom" (John 14:13).

As any girl would do, she turned to her mother and inquired as to what she should ask to receive. Her mother told her to ask for the head of John the Baptist. The daughter went straightaway with haste to the king and asked for the head of John. The king was exceedingly sorry because he did not want to kill John the Baptist but his word was out. Because of his oath, he could not reject her request.

Therefore, the king sent an executioner to bring back the head of John. He went and beheaded John who was already in prison and returned with the head of John on a dish and gave it to the girl, who then gave it to her mother. When the disciples of John heard about his death, they came and took away his body and laid it in a tomb.

Did you know that there is a language of the dead that can speak after the body has been buried? The dead speak in a language that nobody can hear except that one individual. It seems that everywhere King Herod went he could hear the voice of John the Baptist saying, "It is not lawful for you to have your brother, Phillip's wife" (Matt. 14:4).

History, both sacred and profane, is but a voice from the dead. It is the record of the life stories of humankind. Every time we read them, they speak anew to us. They serve to bring back the personality and figure of those who performed those acts.

Many a man and woman would have gone astray long ago if it were not for the voice of a sainted mother. Although she has crossed the mystic river, her voice can be heard above the roaring mist of sin. When she speaks her language, it will often bring the wanderer home.

The dead speak a carefree language. Their language is not the involvement of transpiring events characterizing a dynamic present, but rather the quietude of an inactive past.

In the Old Testament, Genesis 4, there were two brothers who gave to God out of their harvests. These brothers were Cain and Abel. Abel was a keeper of sheep and Cain was a tiller of the ground. When time came for them to make offerings unto the Lord, Cain was not careful in bringing the best of the fruit of the ground to present to the Lord. But Abel took special pains to get the very best among his flock to give unto the Lord. God admired the gift of Abel but not the gift of Cain.

The impact incident to this failure so dwarfed Cain's soul that he heads the murder list in human society. He rises up and kills his brother, Abel. The Lord knew everything; however, he did ask Cain, "Where is Abel, your brother?" Cain replied, "I do not know. Am I my brother's keeper?" The Lord then said,

"What have you done? The voice of your brother's blood cries out to Me from the ground" (Gen. 4:9). Abel is dead but his blood was crying out from the ground.

When you are weary and feeling like quitting, if you would listen, you may be able to hear prophet Isaiah telling you to wait on the Lord, "But those who wait on the Lord shall renew their strength; they shall mount up with wings like eagles, they shall run and not be weary; they shall walk and not faint" (Isa. 40:31).

When people do evil things against you and all they can to make you unhappy, if you would just listen, you could probably hear David speaking to you, "Fret not thyself because of evildoers, nor be envious of the workers of iniquity. Because they shall soon be cut down like grass, and wither as the green herb. But you trust in the Lord and do good; so shall thou dwell in the land, and verily thou shall be fed" (Ps. 37:1–3).

Sometimes I get a chance to listen to Paul. He may say that "if you openly admit by your own mouth that Jesus Christ is the Lord, and if you believe in your own heart that God raised him from the dead, you will be saved, for with the heart man believeth unto righteousness; and with the mouth confession is made unto salvation." For the Scripture says,

> whosoever believeth on him shall not be ashamed. For there is no difference between the Jew and the Greek: for the same Lord over all is rich unto all that call upon him. For whosoever shall call upon the name of the Lord shall be saved. How then shall they call on him in whom they have not believed? And how shall they believe in him of whom they have not heard? And how shall they hear without a preacher? And how shall they preach, except they be sent? (Rom. 10:11–15a).

Sometimes when I am in the spirit, I could visualize that I am having a meeting not only with the apostle Paul, but with John Newton, Isaac Watts, and others.

When I become concerned about this journey, I think about John Newton who started a conversation by reminding us:

How sweet the name of Jesus sounds
In a believer's ear!
It soothes his sorrows, heals his wounds
And drives away his fear.

Fannie Crosby came into the conversation by relating her story:

Blessed assurance Jesus is mine!
O what a foretaste of glory divine!
Heir of Salvation, purchase of God,
Born of his spirit, washed in His blood.
This is my story, this is my song,
Praising my Savior all the day long.

Paul was there and talked about what the Lord has in store for his faithful: "Eye has not seen, nor had ear heard, neither have entered into the heart of man, the things which God has prepared for them that love him" (1 Cor. 2:9).

However, the real thing that keeps me going comes from one who is alive. He is the one who called and commissioned me to preach the Gospel more than fifty years ago. I have tried to be obedient to that divine call. I have tried very hard to follow the "lead of the Spirit of God."

"Inasmuch as you have done it unto one of the least of these my brethren, you have done it unto me."

Matthew 25:40b

CHAPTER THREE

The Future of Black Institutions of Higher Education

One of the finest things that has happened to the historic Black institutions was the founding of the United Negro College Fund, Incorporated, which gives annual support to those Negro educational institutions founded before 1945. Since that time, at least one of the original recipients, Bishop College, has closed its doors.

Of course, the Negroes of fifty years ago were happy to get such support from many persons who wanted to help educate Negro minds. They chose the slogan, "A mind is a terrible thing to waste." The questions that still need to be answered are:

1. Have Blacks reached the conclusion that there is no need for the founding of any new institutions while other races of people are opening new schools?
2. Why do Blacks have to limit their support to the historic institutions of higher education when others are founding new educational institutions?
3. Why do we have to wait until an educational institution is fully accredited before we give it any help?

There is the Baptist Seminary of Richmond which was founded in Richmond, Virginia, and is being funded by churches and conventions. This seminary received funds long before it was accredited. Of course, it is very hard and seemingly impossible for an institution to pull itself towards full accreditation without help from strong organizations. Why would anyone say to a baby, We will give you some breakfast when you come to the table? The baby would soon die because the baby needs the nutrition from the food in order to have enough strength to get to the table. Hence, why would anyone say to a new school, We will give you some help when you become fully accredited? Many times that school will be able to merit accreditation only if it had the needed funds.

Of course, no school should expect to receive funds from organizations just because a request has been made. The schools desiring to get some help from organizations should permit these organizations to come to the campus and observe what is going on before the funds are given. Then, members from the organizations can return at a later date to see if the school has used the funds wisely.

Some things that the organizations need to check are:

Give an examination of the CEO of the school.
Check his/her record with funds that this CEO has managed in other positions that he/she has held. How well did he/she do at that other institution?
Check the list of the faculty members and their character and training.
Check on the graduates and see how well they are doing.

These are some of the tests that the Richmond Virginia Seminary will pass with flying colors.

"Be kind one to another; be understanding. Be as ready to forgive others as God for Christ's sake has forgiven you."

Ephesians 4:32 PHILLIPS MODERN ENGLISH TRANSLATION

CHAPTER FOUR

He's Down—Don't Kick Him, Help Him Up

There are times when persons who have worked very hard to climb to the top of the ladder have permitted greed and lust to break the rounds which then causes them to fall to the bottom. Seldom can we predict when these falls will come but various lifestyles have their own conclusions. The following message was preached from the pulpit of the Cedar Street Baptist Church of God:

Even when one is the cause of his downfall, it's no reason for those who are standing to kick him. The floors of life are very slippery and it is easier to fall than to get up. Satan has greased the pathway and made it hard for one to keep from falling. Just as banana peels thrown onto the sidewalk can easily cause one to slip and fall, the peelings from greed and lust are thrown all along the sidewalks of life; many have already fallen. Therefore, one has to be very careful, lest he slips on the multiplicities of worldly pleasures. Even in a worldly sport such as boxing, the referee will not permit one boxer to hit the other boxer while he is down.

When I was a boy in the hills of Roanoke, Virginia, I found much pleasure in going to the movies on Saturdays and seeing those old westerns. Of course, in those days, there were the good guys and the bad guys. I noticed that during the fights between the cowboys one would knock the other down. However, you would not see a cowboy hitting the other man while he was down. After having knocked the other cowboy down, he would pick him up, and then knock him down again.

Galatians 6:1 says, "Dear Brothers, if a man is overcome by some sin, you who are Christians should gently and humbly help him back onto the right path, remembering that next time it might be one of you who is in the wrong."

Now who are the Christians? The Christians are the ones who have put on the clean clothes of the new life which was made by God's design for righteousness and the holiness which is no illusion.

"Therefore if any man be in Christ, he is a new creature: old things are passed away; behold, all things are become new" (2 Cor. 5:17).

One of the main things seen in this new person is kindness: "Be kind one to another" (Eph. 4:32a). It is all right to be tender-hearted since it gives strength for forgiving one another. Paul attempts to clarify by saying, "Even as God for Christ's sake has forgiven you" (Eph. 4:32b).

I suppose, the first thing we ought to say is that the Christian goal is unattainable in the flesh. We may live and act better than many persons, but we can always be better than we are. We can all improve.

We may love our neighbors. But when it is added that we should love our neighbors as we love ourselves, that is when we have the true test. We all agree that the Ten Commandments are easier to live up to than the Sermon on the Mount. The rich, young ruler said that he had observed all the commandments from his youth onwards. Yet, when confronted with the challenge of the Gospel, he felt it was too much for him. Therefore, he went away sorrowfully.

Sometimes I hear people talking about how much they have done for the local church program and how great they seem to be. If anyone could boast, it would have been the apostle Paul. Yet, I can hear Paul as he speaks in God's Holy Word, "Brethren, I count not myself to have apprehended; but this one thing I do, forgetting those things which are behind, and reaching forth unto those things which are before, I press toward the mark for the prize of the high calling of God in Christ Jesus" (Phil. 3:14). We might say that Christianity does present us with an ever-receding goal.

We ask the question, "What is forgiveness anyway?" Forgiveness is essential to the Christian faith. We should try to cleanse our hearts and minds by forgiving those who have wronged us or those who we think have wronged us.

Forgiveness means to set aside revenge and retaliation. When we forgive, we never seek an opportunity to strike back at the person whom we have forgiven. To forgive a person is to restore that person into fellowship again. The father forgave the prodigal son, even after the son had received his share from the father's goods and spent all in riotous living. Yet, when the son returned home, there was no rebuke from the father. In fact, the father ran to meet him and fell on his neck kissing him.

You remember Saul and David. Saul was jealous of David for no reason other than the fact that David was popular with the people. The people were heard singing, that "Saul hath slain his thousands, and David his ten thousands" (1 Sam. 18:7). This favoritism angered Saul so much that he set out to find David and kill him. Yet, during this time, David had two opportunities to destroy Saul, but David refused both times.

Hosea continued to love an unfaithful wife and forgave her each time that she played the harlot. He would get her from great whoredom and bring her back home (Hos. 1:2).

The supreme example of forgiveness is exemplified by Jesus himself. While He was dying on the cross, He could ask His

Father to forgive those who were His enemies because He knew that they were ignorant and did not know what they were doing. The reason we should forgive is because every man and every woman wants others to forgive him or her. It does not matter how wrong one has been, he or she wants forgiveness. In fact, I have never met a person who did not want forgiveness for the wrongs or the sins he or she has committed.

Nobody really wants justice when one has wronged a neighbor or committed a wrong deed against society. He or she wants mercy and forgiveness; this person wants no part of justice when he or she is wrong. The man who takes the life of another person wants to be forgiven by the relatives and friends of the one whose life he has taken. Therefore, if a person has wronged you and wants forgiveness, good sportsmanship, if nothing else, would require that you forgive him or her because you would like to be forgiven for the wrongs you have done.

We don't live in a perfect world. Our parents are not perfect. Our children are not perfect. I don't know of any perfect marriages. In fact, I have discovered that there are some mean, jealous, selfish, and unpleasant ways in all the people that I have known. Although every individual has missed the mark of perfection, we press on to that ever-receding goal. Even after we have put on the new man, Satan does not leave us alone. Did you think that when you made the promise "that you would serve the Lord until you died" Satan would have said, Well, the Lord has him now, therefore, I will leave him alone? In fact, when you commit yourself to the Lord, Satan will try harder to conquer you when you are trying to do what is right.

I know there are a whole lot of things that many of us would not dare to do. But this should not put us out of touch with those who need us. We have no right to brag about how righteous we are. I believe that the Pharisee told the truth in the temple that day. He said he was unlike other men, that he fasted twice a week, and gave his tithe on all his possessions. He told the truth;

he did do all of that. However, the self-righteousness of his prayer caused Jesus to think more of the Publican than the Pharisee, who had lived so righteously. All the Publican said in his prayer was, "Lord, have mercy on me a sinner" (Luke 18:13).

The rich man in Luke 16:19 was not guilty of any of the seven deadly sins. He went to Hell because he failed to see poor Lazarus at his gate. He had an arm of wealth strong enough to have picked up Lazarus. He was very rich, clothing himself in purple and fine linen and faring sumptuously every day. Instead of picking up the poor man by giving him some food to eat, he psychologically kicked him by turning the dogs on him. If we are to follow our Master, we are to forgive those who we know are our enemies. Jesus said,

> Love your enemies and bless them that curse you, do good to them that hate you, and pray for them which despitefully use you and persecute you; that you may be the children of your Heavenly Father which is in heaven; for God makes His sun to rise on the evil and on the good, and sends his rain on the just and on the unjust. (Matt. 5:44)

Our calculating minds would raise questions about the limits of forgiveness. The rational mind would say, How much are we required to accept before we put the brakes on? Do we have to take the same insults over and over again from the same person?

Well, you could stay out of that person's presence. But the plain truth is, according to God's Word, there is no limit as can be revealed by explaining what to do when one man trespasses against you. Do you remember Peter's question to Jesus? Peter asked, "Lord, how often shall my brother sin against me, and I forgive him?"(Matt. 18:21). Peter believed seven to be the perfect number, therefore, he felt that seven should be the limit. Jesus responded, "No, Peter, not seven times but seventy times seven" (Matt. 18:22). Though not a thousand, or a million times,

Jesus was still telling Peter not to count the times. Don't go around with a notepad in your pocket, writing down the number of times a person has wronged you. Instead, every time they wrong you, forgive them. Jesus is telling us not to use arithmetic.

The reason why many people cannot forgive is that the old man is still in charge. The old man must be crucified with Christ to prevent us from serving sin. This does not mean that the flesh, the old nature, is ever eliminated in this life. We do not get rid of the old nature, but we are not to live in it; that is, we are not to allow it to control our lives. Satan never leaves us. He tries to deceive every mind. If it were left to Satan, he would burn every Bible and destroy every church gathering. Satan dislikes the truth and those who rejoice in the Lord. He lurks behind every corner and every door. He sneaks through every place and rushes down every roadway and pathway. He hates when one sinner comes to Christ and wants to misguide the lives of youth. Satan is a terrible person.

One may ask the question, How can we be kind to one another, be understanding, and be as ready to forgive others like God for Christ's sake has forgiven you? We must admit that we cannot do it on our own. We must have a new nature that is the result of regeneration by the Holy Spirit. Any man in Christ is surely a new creation.

The Christian enjoys many blessings and benefits that those who are not "in Christ" cannot have. There is no other source from which we may be received but "in and through Christ." When we are "in Christ," we are no longer under condemnation because we are not walking after the flesh but rather after the spirit. When we become a new creature in Christ Jesus, we are no longer a servant of sin because we have become a servant of righteousness. We become through this relationship with Christ Jesus spiritually clean because we have been washed and sanctified by His Spirit.

Let's have another look at what Jesus teaches about forgiveness. Jesus had spent the night on the Mount of Olives. After a full night's sleep, the Great Teacher made His way to the training grounds to interpret the word for some eager listeners. It was always a privilege for the people just to sit at the feet of the Master and hear His matchless truths. The people just sat there with their hearts and ears open. His teachings transcended, exceeded, surpassed, and excelled all things. The more one contemplates, meditates, and evaluates the Word of God, the more impossible it becomes to find words that justify the Glory of His Word. In his message, one finds a volume with no limitations, a circle with no circumference, and a depth with no restrictions. The only way the people could learn was by sitting at Jesus' feet. There were no printing presses at that time and no books to be read.

They were having a great worship service, when suddenly while Jesus was teaching, a commotion arose near the edge of the crowd. They could hear the angry shouts from the Scribes and Pharisees rising above the sound of the Master's voice. These men rudely burst in upon the Holy assembly and began their wicked procedure. They missed the meaning of our text, which says, "Be kind one to another, be understanding. Be as ready to forgive others as God for Christ's sake has forgiven you" (Eph. 4:32 PHILLIPS).

These men could not wait until the worship was over. They wanted an answer from Jesus right then. They wanted the privilege to stone a woman who had been caught in adultery. Nothing is said in the story about the woman's background. We do not know if her motive was economic, social, or deliberately sinful. We do not know the woman's attitude toward being reported and caught. Of course, she was embarrassed. She may have been defiant and openly resentful. She may have appeared mad and aggressive. She may have been weeping, or very calm. We do not know.

These Pharisees and the teachers of the Laws of Moses informed Jesus, "Teacher, this woman was caught sleeping with a man, who isn't her husband. The law of Moses teaches that a woman like this should be stoned to death! What do you say?" (John 8:4).

They thought they had Jesus in a dilemma. If Jesus gave them permission to put on a "stone-throwing party," He would have jeopardized His reputation with the people who had heard Him talking about loving one's enemies and doing good towards those who spitefully use you. If He had openly declared that this woman should not be stoned for her sin, or that she should be pardoned and forgiven, they would have felt He was teaching to break the Law of Moses and condoning the sin of adultery.

They were ready for a stone-throwing party. I like to go to a birthday party or an anniversary party where I can have some fun. But when you are getting ready to have a "stone-throwing party," where you try to crucify a person for doing some wrong, please don't invite me to that kind of party because I cannot join you in throwing stones; I live in a glass house and I am afraid one of those rocks will ricochet.

Thank God, Jesus could look through them and discern their every thought and purpose. He knew their plan was to catch and expose him, bringing him into collision with the Roman law. Therefore, Jesus refused to argue with His enemies. He caught these accusers with a sudden move that immediately floored them.

John stated that Jesus did not answer the accusers at all. My Jesus simply stooped down and began to write on the sand with his finger as though he had not heard them. Of course, this made them so uncomfortable that they continued to press Jesus for an answer. "Now the law of Moses commanded us to stone such, What do you say about her?" (John 8:5 RSV). They wanted to test Jesus and bring some charge against him.

Finally, Jesus stood up and said, "If any of you have never sinned, then go ahead and throw the first stone at her!" (John 8:7). He wanted the one without sin to be the first to throw a stone. We need a sinless individual to throw the first stone.

Again Jesus stooped down and wrote some more on the ground. They heard Jesus say, "If any of you have never sinned" (John 8:7a). They began to think of their faults. After carefully thinking over their whole lives, they began to walk away slowly, one by one. It is said that the senior citizens walked away first then the parents and finally the children until everybody had gone. At last, Jesus and the woman were there alone. Jesus stood up and asked her, "Where is everyone? Isn't there anybody left to accuse you?" "No Sir," the woman answered. Jesus told her, "I am not going to accuse you either. You may go now, but don't sin anymore" (John 8:10).

Our Evening Prayer should be:

> If I have wounded any soul today,
> If have caused one foot to go astray,
> If I have walked in my own wilful way,
> Dear Lord, forgive.

"Behold, how good and pleasant it is for brethren to dwell together in unity!"
Psalms 133:1

CHAPTER FIVE

Cedar Street's Family Nights

As I mentioned in my previous book, *Just As He Promised*, Cedar Street had many things that I found very interesting when I became the pastor in 1955. One of these was the monthly Family Nights in which the talented members of Cedar Street would have an opportunity to express their special gifts. The membership of Cedar Street was not large, therefore, most of the time, it was the same persons leading the night of fun.

Usually, Miss Mary McPherson or Mrs. Estelle Jones, who served as the Mistress of Ceremony, led the way. Of course, Mrs. Ruth Wilson was at the piano or organ to accompany any person with a musical selection. The musical talents included duets by Miss Coretha Seaborn and Mrs. Bertha Ellison, and Mr. and Mrs. Ivory Roots, and a solo by Mr. Clifford C. Jones. There would always be readings by Deacon Andrew C. Epps Sr., Mrs. Delores Braxton, and Mrs. Alma Dean. Mrs. Florence Cosby or Miss Dorothy Nelson would give the welcome address to the few invited guests present. The devotions were led by one of the deacons, Meredith Davis, James Wright, or Walter Green. These Family Nights were very enjoyable and interesting for

Sugar and me. I was young and could attend every activity sponsored by the church. I was there for my remarks, which ended up almost the same, expressing my appreciation to those who had participated.

The Talent Night would always end with a fellowship meal. At this point, Sugar and I began to put on a few extra pounds that have since been hard to take off.

"The stranger did not lodge in the street: but I opened my doors to the traveller."
Job 31:32

CHAPTER SIX

Courtesy In Entertaining Visiting Pastors

During my early ministry, I thought that when a pastor friend would come by Cedar Street on a Sunday morning I owed him the courtesy of inviting him to bring the gospel message. This was especially true during the summer when pastors would have a month's vacation. Cedar Street was a popular church in the minds of many preachers. I felt that a pastor was not hospitable if he did not make the offer for the guest to preach. Many times, a pastor who had had a guest preacher the previous Sunday would feel the need to inform the visiting preacher why the pastor was obligated to preach that Sunday.

The offer was often made because that pastor wanted the same to be extended to him. The pastors' salaries were so low that many of them used their vacation periods to visit a different church each Sunday hoping the pastor would let them preach. I have heard some preachers say, "I visited my friend of many years and he did not extend the invitation to me to bring the morning's message. How selfish can a preacher be when his friend comes by? I would have let him preach if he had come to my church and would have taken up a special offering for him as guest preacher."

During those early years, I went to churches with a sermon in my pocket. I wanted to be prepared if the opportunity was extended. Somehow, I felt all right if the pastor recognized me as the pastor of Cedar Street Baptist Church in Richmond and then brought the message himself. Cedar Street had always given me a livable income. Therefore, I was glad to sit in the congregation and hear a soul-stirring sermon from the pastor. Sometimes I found myself trying to justify to a guest pastor visiting Cedar Street while on his vacation why I needed to preach that morning. I can hear myself now saying, "Reverend, I would ask you to preach, but I have had too many guest preachers this summer that I must preach today myself." I have had those who wanted to preach say to me, "Ben, they can hear you next Sunday."

After I matured more, I came to believe that it is the pastor's obligation to feed his flock. Many Sunday mornings I have been in the office before worship time when the telephone rings and the question is asked, "Is Dr. Robertson preaching this morning?" If the answer is affirmative, they would come on to church; if negative, they would visit another church or stay home. It does not bother me when a preacher visits our Divine Worship, I usually preach because I have come prepared to preach. Of course, the guest preacher would stir the congregation because every preacher has a few sermons that they have preached so often that it becomes natural for them.

Since our television and radio broadcasts are heard each Sunday, I am in the pulpit of Cedar Street about fifty Sundays a year. We do have special Sundays in which we have guest preachers, but I am always there in the pulpit with them. Sugar and I help to entertain the preachers and their wives while they are staying in Richmond as our guests. I do not recommend that a preacher give as much time in the pulpit as I give because he/she will be invited to be the guest preacher at other churches on Sunday mornings. I am able to be in the pulpit almost every

Sunday of the year because we take only a few days for vacation. After about four or five days in a vacation place, Sugar and I usually have had enough and want to go home. Therefore, we can leave home on a Sunday afternoon and return home on Friday night after a fine vacation. In recent years, I have accepted preaching engagements to serve during the week or on Sunday afternoons or nights. I don't think it's selfish if I enjoy preaching at Cedar Street. I usually take a Sunday during the month of July when the church plans a trip to some vacation spot. Many times when preachers invite me and I cannot come, they will ask me to give them a time when I could come. Many times, it can be a good vacation spot. One year, we were in Nassau, in the Bahamas, and I preached at the Mt. Calvary Baptist Church, with Dr. McPhee, Pastor. Another year, we were in Orlando, Florida, at the Mt. Pleasant Baptist Church, with Dr. W. A. Prince Jr., Pastor. Yet, another year, we were back in Nassau at the Mt. Carey Baptist Church, with Dr. Phillip Rahming, Pastor. Of course, I don't want anyone to think that I am like this lady in Boston who did not travel. People knew that she never left Boston. Therefore, one day she was asked why she did not travel. Her simple reply was, "I am already here."

I have discovered that one cannot build a church running all over the country on Sunday mornings. Since I am usually at Cedar Street on Sunday mornings and usually preaching, we do not get those calls asking, "Who's preaching?" It is also true that since the people know the pastor will be there, the church is comfortably filled each Sunday during the year.

Have you ever been dining in a restaurant when a person comes in from the outside and reaches to shake your hand? I suggest to the approaching person to wait until the person dining extends his/her hand. The average handshaking person shakes a whole lot of hands in a day. One never knows how many of those persons had clean hands. Germs are frequently transmitted by a handshake. The proper thing to do when you approach a person who is dining is to carry on a conversation without a handshake. Your hands may have been washed, but what about those others whose hands you have shaken.

I have not been able to accept the new trend of men sitting at the table with their hats on. I still believe that a man should take his hat off in an elevator and at the table while dining.

"But if we are led by the Spirit, we are not under the law."
Galatians 5:18

CHAPTER SEVEN

Minister's Wife Speaks

Mrs. Dolores W. Robertson

I have been with my husband because the Spirit of God has been leading me to help him in whatever way that I can to do the work of the Master. The law is not necessary when one is led by God's Spirit because the Spirit teaches as it leads. Many times, the Spirit of God works through those in whose care we are entrusted.

My mother, Jeanette Holmes, and my grandmother, Alberta Holloway, had great influence upon my early childhood. Both of them were dedicated Christian women and taught me to be ladylike regardless of the circumstance. They taught me that a young lady does not fight or argue on the street. I believed them. Therefore, many times my lunch was taken away from me without a struggle on my part. My mother would prepare my lunch, thinking that I was eating it. So many times, I didn't even know what was in the lunch because the larger girls would take it from me. I was not a very large child. In fact, I was small when smallness was not appreciated as it is today.

I would get home from school before my mother could get there from work. My mother gave me a key and told me to go in and do my homework. After studying for a while, I would go

Mrs. Dolores "Sugar" Robertson

to the window and watch for the bus to stop and Mama would get off. Oh, the thrill that came to my heart when I would see her coming. I knew, then, that we would have something nice to talk about. We didn't have a television but we had our radio. So we listened to music. She taught me to listen to music she considered to be soft and soothing. This type of music helped me to appreciate the hymns and anthems that were sung at Second Baptist Church under the pastorate of the late Dr. Joseph T. Hill. Then, I went to Virginia Union University and became a member of the university choir, which was directed by Professor William Goodwin. I did not appreciate Gospel music until I was married and my husband and I came to Cedar Street Baptist Church of God.

I feel that great credit should be given to a minister who makes sure his wife is taken care of and properly respected. I have had no problem in this respect. For "Daddy" has always looked out for me. We would not be anywhere for very long without everybody knowing that his "Sugar" was there. Because we were special to each other, he felt that I was special to everybody. He always made me feel that I was wanted and loved.

When I graduated from Virginia Union University, I wanted to go immediately and apply for a teaching position. But Benjamin had the "old fashioned Roanoke" idea that the preacher's wife should not have an outside job. My husband does not love money but he understands good business and has been an excellent provider for Benjamin Jr. and me. I guess I fall in with the other wives who think that their husbands understand the business world. However, once I sat down with him and showed how I could help financially, he quickly fell for it. Therefore, for thirty-one years, I worked at the Whitcomb Court Elementary School.

Our marriage has been pleasant because we have tried to do what we can to help each other. As for me, I have never been involved in any disturbance at the church, but everybody knows where I stand. I stand right by his side while he does the battling. There is no need for me to get involved because he is capable of taking care of himself. I have sometimes wondered to myself how is he going to get out of this. But when the battle is over and the dust has subsided, "Daddy" was always standing tall.

I recognized anew the strength of this man whom I had married when the life of our son, Benjamin Jr., came to a sudden end. Of course, it was a beautiful hot July day but it became a cold, dark day for us. He came through as a husband, friend, and one who appeared to understand death. His strong faith in the resurrection helped my own faith in the resurrection to increase greatly. Dr. C. L. Evans called and recommended that I should talk with another pastor. He felt that Benjamin was too involved in the same bereavement that he could not help me. He suggested that I should talk with either Dr. Robert L. Taylor or Dr. E. D. McCreary Jr. I appreciated Dr. Evans's interest in my moments of mourning, but Benjamin and I were getting ourselves together quite quickly. We began to thank God for the eighteen years we had Benjamin Jr. with us. Of course, Benjamin Jr. and I were very close but his leaving was filled by a closer walk with Jesus and the inspiration of a caring husband.

My mother instilled in me the need to be a lady in all situations. I have tried to obey her advice and be the person whom God wanted me to be. However, there have been times when I had to express myself very frankly to some persons because it seemed as if there was only one way by which they could understand. Most of the time, I have been respected for who I have tried to be. I have truly enjoyed these forty-five years as a pastor's wife.

—Dolores "Sugar" Robertson
Wife of Benjamin W. Robertson Sr.

"Therefore, brethren, seek out from among you seven men of good reputation, full of the Holy Spirit and wisdom, whom we may appoint over this business."

Acts 6:3

CHAPTER EIGHT

The New Trend in Church Officials

There is a growing trend toward the elimination of the deacons and trustees as we have known them in the past. Maybe some of it has been caused by many members of the Board of Deacons acting as if God had left them solely in charge of the administration of the local church. Some have regarded the pastor as a hired servant who must listen to the dictates of the boards. There have been times when a pastor has felt that the congregation would follow his recommendation, but the strong persons on the Deacon and Trustee Boards have blocked it in a meeting. Many times peace-loving members never get the opportunity to express their desires because of such strong board members.

There have been jokes about the Deacon's prayer. The deacon would pray to God and ask God to make the preacher humble while they kept him poor.

For years, there was a flat fee of five dollars for preachers who delivered the eulogy at funerals. With the deacons and trustees controlling the finances of the church, the pastor was one of the lowest paid persons in the community. Yet, he was expected to lead in giving to the church's drive and buy candy from every child who was selling it. Many of the pastors had to conduct revivals, preach while on vacation, and take as many outside engagements as they could get for "financial survival." He was not expected to buy an expensive home or car. The pastor of yesteryear had to remain as pastor of a church long after his abilities declined because these churches provided no retirement for him.

A few persons of the church who saw the financial need of the pastor's family organized what is known as the Pastor's Aid Society. When I came to Cedar Street, Ms. Missouri Jackson and a few others organized pastor's aid for me. They operated about six months and made some nice presentations to Sugar and me. However, the name was embarrassing for me because it made me feel as if I were begging. I felt that Cedar Street owed me a salary with which Sugar and I could live comfortably. Therefore, I disbanded this aid society and met with the officers concerning my salary. The church was growing so rapidly that it was not a problem for them to give me a salary that was larger than most Virginia pastors. It appeared that the officers of Cedar Street wanted their pastor to be properly cared for by those whom he served.

However, we must recognize that all churches were not as fortunate as Cedar Street to have deacons and trustees who knew that a pastor with less problems of his own could give better service to the parishioners. Therefore, the trend of the nineties seems to have been for preachers to pull out of an established congregation, take as many members who would follow him, and establish a church of his liking. These new churches have been named many different names. In my observation, there are three things that each of these new congregations share regardless of their names. First, they have made it crystal clear that they should have no deacons, and if there are deacons, they will be appointed by the pastor to serve at his pleasure. Second, there are no Boards of Trustees since the trustees will be appointed by the pastor only to satisfy the legal matters of the court. Third, the members do not ride around in big cars, build expensive houses, or forget the church. Therefore, each member remains a "tither." As stated previously, tithing is the proper way to carry on God's program. The Bible teaches tithe and offerings.

Now there are other things that the new trend of church operation has. For an honest pastor, this system may work well. He is in charge of the administrative and spiritual work of the church. There is nothing wrong with the pastor leading the congregation; this is his biblical charge. However, by having no deacons or trustees and all tithers, it leaves much room for gross dishonesty. Since the church has certain taxable exemption rights, a pastor with no one to check him could rob the tithe box under the title of salary and gifts.

The next question which comes up is, "Who determines if a member is tithing or not?" Will the pastor or his appointee actually become involved in checking how much a person makes to determine his or her tithe?

In talking with many founders of new movements, I discovered that church policies do not give room for the dismissal of the pastor under any condition. I am merely calling attention to this fact. I have no authority to say what is right or what is wrong. It seems as if these founding pastors have secured their authority within these movements for a long, long time. This security is cemented by placing the wife as co-pastor and other relatives in positions of authority. As I have stated before, I am in no position to criticize what they have done because I have never worn their shoes. I have been the pastor of Cedar Street since 1955 and have been seriously challenged only once. This challenge came in 1987 and the congregation supported me by giving me more than 90 percent of the vote and an authority far above the average Baptist pastor.

After almost half a century with the same congregation, I must confess that I really need our current deacons and trustees. They know how to treat a pastor and make him feel wanted and respected. Having known the deacons at First Union Baptist Church in Richmond in 1952, the deacons at Piney Grove Baptist Church in Virginia Beach in 1953, and the deacons at Cedar Street since 1955, I would not want to be pastor of a church without deacons and trustees.

"Then said Jesus, Father, forgive them, for they know not what they do."
Luke 23:34

CHAPTER NINE

Forgiven Without Asking

THE FIRST EXPRESSION FROM THE CROSS

This is the first expression of Jesus from the Cross which is the final day of the Passion Week. The significance of the Passion Week is set to the principles of a beautiful seven-act drama. Just as each of the days of the week has a distinct message, so do the seven expressions from the cross have special meanings to help understand Jesus' compassion and love even in the hour of death.

In order to fully understand the cross, we must glance at the actions of Jesus during Passion Week in which He was fully inflamed with zeal for God's cause, consuming the last drops of His personal desire. He had now completely forgotten self; His will was lost in the great Will of God.

This was the only way that His disciples could account for the boldness of His actions in cleansing the Temple. The Passion Week drama opens with the bold assertion of Jesus to be King of the Jews. Up until this point, Jesus had largely concealed His claim to be the Messiah or even to be the King of the Jews. That is why He wanted some of His miracles to be performed in secrecy. He, therefore, openly proclaimed Himself the Messiah and refused to still the Hosannas of the crowd who announced Him as the Messianic King.

On His way out of the city on Monday, the incident of the fruitless fig tree takes place. The tree which represented the Jewish nation has leaves but no fruit.

Tuesday was a day crowded with transpiring events. Here in the Temple, He taught a lesson of supreme trust.

Wednesday was spent in retirement. The record is silent for this day. However, it is reasonable to suppose that this day was spent in the review of what had happened and what will happen in the world with the Twelve.

Thursday marks the institution of the Last Supper which ended with a sad occasion. However, there is that beautiful prayer which comes after the supper.

Now, we gather here on Friday and the same question comes to the minds of many, "Why the cross?"

The people in Jesus' time on earth never intended for the cross of Christ to be a thing of beauty, or a place of peace and joy, or a place of honor and comfort. They never intended for the cross to become the "hope" of a lost, sinful, wicked, and ungodly world.

So we come unto the place that is called the skull, the "Calvary" or "Golgatha" which literally means "the place of the skull."

Here was a man who was not guilty of any sin. Yet, the Jews took Him to Pilate to be judged guilty. We already know that only the Roman government could pronounce the death penalty. Jesus had been charged with claiming to be king. He was charged as a revolutionist because they felt that Jesus had incited the people not to pay taxes.

Jesus is now hanging on the cross. Here is a man whose heart had gone out through deeds of love toward the suffering and sorrowing of humanity. Here is a man who was moved with compassion for the unloved. Here is a man whose disciple's benediction of his life was "that he went about doing good."

Here we are standing at the foot of the cross, waiting to hear what this man on the center cross had to say. We can hear the profanity from the malefactor but we haven't heard a word from this strange man. This man claimed to have done no wrong, well, what is he doing up here anyway?

His first words were, "Father, forgive them, for they know not what they do" (Luke 23:34). Many times we have heard this interpreted to mean that Jesus was talking about those who were casting lots for His garments. Of course, I am sure that He had them in mind. But listen to the rulers respond, "He saved others, let Him save Himself, if he be Christ, the chosen of God" (Luke 23:35). Then the soldiers are mentioned mocking Him and offering Him vinegar. I am sure that he meant forgiveness for all of them. Our interpretation is often not as inclusive as what I believe the Savior wanted it to be.

I believe that Jesus was praying for more than those gamblers who were dividing his garments and casting lots. Make no mistake he meant the gamblers but not them exclusively. If he meant only them, he would have been more specific by saying something like, "Father, forgive these gamblers for they know not what they are doing." Or he could have said, "Father, forgive these people who are crucifying me." If the ones whom Jesus wanted the Father to forgive were the ones right at the cross, he would have said "these" because "these" refers to a particular group.

Do you remember that previous Sunday when some of the Pharisees wanted Jesus to rebuke that Palm Sunday cheering squad? The disciples of Jesus were right there and Jesus referred to the disciples as these. "I tell you that, if these hold their peace, the stones would immediately cry out" (Luke 19:40).

When Jesus came to the city of Samaria, he was weary from his journey. Therefore, he sat down on Jacob's well. A woman of Samaria came to draw some water from the well. John records that Jesus said to this particular woman, "Give me to drink." Jesus was asking this Samaritan woman to give Him a drink of water. Listen to her reply, "How is it that you, being a Jew, ask a drink of me who is a woman of Samaria?" (John 4:10).

If Jesus had not asked this particular woman for a drink, no one knows what might have happened. If He had not asked it of her, the angels in heaven might have departed from the Celestial City, coming to the banks of glory and leading those heavenly servants who had been standing in attention since the dawn of Creation towards action. They would have set up a spring of eternal water flowing from the clouds. But Jesus individualized His request by asking this woman who had come to the well to give Him some water.

When Lazarus was dead, Jesus came to call him back to life. Jesus came to the grave calling him by his name. If Jesus had stood at the grave and had just said "Come forth" without calling the name of the person whom He had come to raise, all the graves would have probably opened and all the dead would have gotten up and come out of their graves. But Jesus just wanted Lazarus to come forth. Therefore, He individualized it by calling Lazarus by name, "Lazarus, come forth." John said that Lazarus came forth with his hands and feet bound with grave clothes. Jesus then said, "Loose him and let him go" (John 11:43).

Somehow, I just believe that Jesus was inclusive in His prayer of forgiveness when He said, "Father, forgive them." I might ask, "What *them*?" If I was to say "these," you would look for something that was near us. If I was to say "those," you would look for something that is away from us. But when we say "them," you don't know where to look for "them." "Them" can refer to something close up or far away. "Them" can be above or below us. "Them" could be on the right or the left side.

I believe that Jesus peeped through the vicissitude of time to see nations rejecting God's only begotten Son and said, "Father, forgive them." He saw worlds dying and going to hell and said,

"Father, forgive them." He saw those with hearts of sin refusing to repent.

He saw multitudes of souls that nobody but He could redeem and said, "Father, forgive them." He saw the guilty and said, "Father, forgive them." He saw hands stained with innocent blood and said, "Father, forgive them." He heard lying and deceitful tongues and said, "Father, forgive them." He saw men and women with lustful and greedy eyes and said, "Father, forgive them." He saw corrupt and wicked individuals with proud, arrogant attitudes and cold hearts and said, "Father, forgive them."

He saw gamblers, criminals at their crimes, harlots at their business, alcoholics at the bottle and said, "Father, forgive them." He saw all the thieves who were hiding, crooks who were cheating, fugitives that were running, murderers who were killing, and said, "Father, forgive them."

He saw hypocrites who were pretending, lying politicians, persons preaching who have never been called or anointed, deacons who have never given up their former lives, choir members who think more of their singing than their salvation, coldhearted church members who hate to see others rejoicing in the worship services, and said, "Father, forgive them."

He saw ungrateful persons whom God had blessed with reasonable portions of health and strength fail to know who gave them food to eat, peace of mind, a good job, a house to live in, a car to ride in, and a good mate and said, "Father, forgive them."

I close by asking God to use me for whatever he wants me to do.

Use me Lord, in your service
Draw me nearer every day,
I am willing, Lord, to run all the way.
If I falter while I am trying
Don't be angry, let me stay

I will be willing, Lord, to run all the way.
Pained by heartache, scorned by loved ones
A little sunshine, now and then,
There are mountains in my life so hard to climb,
But I promised God that I'll keep climbing
If He will only let me in
I will be willing, Lord, to run all the way.

Wasted days are now behind me
My evening sun is sinking fast
Every moment brings me nearer to the end
I will hurry in thy service if you only let me in.

When I have done my best in service
And there is nothing that I can do.
Just a weary, tired pilgrim, sad and alone,
Only linger ever nearer and nearer
While I near my home sweet home.

Many loved ones gone before me
Leave me lonesome as can be
And our parting at the river, I recall
And I promise broken hearted to be faithful to the end.

All the way, all the way, I will be willing to run all the way
If I falter while I am trying,
Don't be angry, let me stay, I will be willing to run all the way.

"And Jesus said unto him, 'Verily I say unto thee, today shalt thou be with me in paradise.'"

Luke 23:43

CHAPTER TEN

There Is No Time to Waste

Dr. Dennis East Thomas

THE SECOND EXPRESSION FROM THE CROSS

Upon close and careful examination of the ministry and the miracles of Jesus Christ, one should observe as well as conclude that our Lord often used the faith of the believer in order to bring to pass unusual signs and wonders in his or her life. Jesus utilized the cooperation, participation, and imagination of believers in order to achieve supernatural signs.

I observe cooperation because it was a man born blind with whom our Lord spat on the ground and made mud. He placed the mud in his eyes and enlisted the blind man's cooperation by instructing him to go and wash. Upon the blind man's cooperation, he came up seeing. I recommend participation because it was a lame man, a paralyzed man who had never walked, whom Jesus told to take up his bed and walk. Upon the lame man's participation in taking up his bed, he witnessed and received his miracle. I suggest imagination because a woman with the issue of blood employed her imagination and just conceived, believing and envisioning her own miracle. She confessed, "I believe if I can just touch the hem of His garment, I shall be made whole" (Matt. 9:21).

With these episodes in mind, let us not discount this dying thief on the cruel cross. He also exercised unusual faith in our Lord and Savior Jesus Christ. As we arrive at the hill of Golgatha, we immediately take note of three distinct men hanging and dying through the process of crucifixion. One man is hanging on the right side, while another is hanging on the wrong side. One man is assured of his entrance into hell, while the other man is trying to gain last minute access into heaven. In the middle, there is a man who has the keys of death and hell in His hands.

That thief on the wrong side became caught up with the crowd. He was moved by the multitudes. He was mocking with the majority. With his words, he reveled against our Lord and with the sneer of sarcasm he exclaimed, "You saved many now save yourself and us." The thief on the right side spoke up and stated, ". . . he has done nothing amiss. When thou comest into thy kingdom, remember me" (Matt. 27:42).

As I personally examine this passage, a perplexing problem is presented. Did this thief on the right side have any previous exposure with the Lord? Had his life shared some prior experience with the Eternal One? Was this encounter at the cross his initial meeting with the Master? This issue makes all the difference in the world regarding how our Lord responded to this thief.

Firstly, let us consider the possibility that this thief knew the Lord prior to this monumental moment. Thus, I would not be surprised or shocked by his soul-saving request: "Lord, when Thou comest into Thy kingdom remember me" (Luke 23:42). If he had seen Christ work miracles, then he would know that there is nothing too hard for Him to do. If he had heard Him preach, then he would know that He was the Way, the Truth, and the Life and that no man comes unto the Father but by Christ Jesus. If he had been familiar with the reputation of Jesus, then he would know that he could do anything but fail. If

Dr. Dennis E. Thomas

he had only bumped into a faithful follower of Christ, then this thief would have known that God shall supply all his needs according to God's riches in glory through Christ Jesus.

If this thief had only seen Christ for himself, he would have known that He was the Door; "by me if any man enter in, he shall be saved!" (John 10:9). He would have known that Jesus was the Good Shepherd who giveth His life for the sheep. He would have known that Jesus was the Resurrection and the Life and that he that believeth in Him, though he were dead, yet shall he live. This condemned man would have already known that whosoever shall call upon the name of the Lord shall be saved.

If this thief knew these things, then such a request would not be out of the ordinary: "Lord, when Thou comest into Thy kingdom, remember me" (Luke 23:42).

Secondly, let us look at this problem from the other side. Consider the possibility that this thief may have never seen, heard, known, or been in the presence of Jesus Christ beforehand. Could it be probable that the ears of the thief had never heard of Him or that the eyes of the thief had never seen him? What if he had no prior experience with Jesus? Unfortunately, there exist countless millions today who have never heard the Gospel of Jesus Christ. This thief represents those fish that are ready to be pulled from the ocean of sin. He reminds us of the harvest that is ripe for picking. We must reach the masses—the men, women, boys, and girls of every birth!

Is it possible that someone can have no previous exposure to the Christ? Was this, in actuality, his initial encounter with Christ? Just imagine the fact that this criminal had to hang on the cross before he became acquainted with the Shelter in the time of storm! If all this were true, then this story becomes one of the greatest demonstrations of faith.

If you look at Jesus at that moment, our Lord appeared to be in no position to make any promises. All he saw with his natural eyes was a man in the same condition as he was. All he saw was a man that was bruised, bleeding, and bloody. All he saw were cuts and gashes. All he saw was a man in misery. All he saw was a man that was wounded on the outside and bruised on the inside. All he saw was a dying man.

Yet, in spite of all that his natural eyes saw, his faith saw something beyond the obvious! This dying thief's faith saw something beyond the nails, something beyond the thorn-crowned brow, something beyond the piercing in the side, something beyond the agony and the misery and said, "Lord, when thou comest into Thy kingdom remember me" (Luke 23:42).

This man never heard the wonderful words of life! This thief was not at the Sea of Galilee nor did he eat of the five loaves and the two fish. In spite of all, this thief looks at Jesus in the present set of circumstances and wishes to be remembered "when Thou comest into Thy kingdom."

I want to know, Where did he get such faith? How could he see a man in the same terminal condition and say "remember me"?

He never heard a sermon. He never saw a miracle. He never saw the blind eyes opened. He never saw the lame man walking. He never saw the blood issue healed. Yet this dying thief could realize the message conveyed so beautifully in the song "There Is a Fountain," by William Cowper, that "There is a fountain filled with blood drawn from Emmanuel's veins; and sinners, plunged beneath that flood lose all their guilty stains. The dying thief rejoiced to see that fountain in his day; and there may I, though vile as he, wash all my sins away."

Lastly, even if this thief had never met the Master before, he had at least been with Jesus long enough to have heard one Word. One Word that he had never heard before. One Word, while everyone else had rejected him. One Word, while everyone else despised him. One Word, while everyone else condemned him. One Word, while everyone else hated him. One Word, while everyone else put him down. One Word, while everyone else threw him down. With this one Word, he heard Jesus say what no one else had ever said. One Word, which was the first Word from the cross: "Father, forgive them for they know not what they do."

Upon hearing that one Word, that only word, that sole Word, enough supernatural faith arose up in him for this thief's heart to say, "I want some of that!" His soul said, "Include me in that forgiven crowd." His eyes saw him by faith in that merciful mass.

For that one Word was a word of forgiveness. That one Word was a word of love. That one Word was a word of mercy. That one Word was a word of compassion. That one Word was inclusive enough for his faith to stimulate cooperation, his spirit to invest in participation, and his soul to plug into imagination: "Lord, when thou comest into Thy kingdom remember me."

Jesus turns His head at the demonstration and expression of this thief's own faith to give us our second word from the cross, "Today." If you can look past the nails, then Today. If you can believe past the bruises, then Today. If you can cooperate even in the midst of your own crucifixion, then Today. If you can participate in the midst of your own pain, then Today. If you can imagine even in the midst of your own agony and misery, then "Today, thou shall be with Me in Paradise" (Luke 23:43).

Jesus was impressed with this man's faith to see Him as the Messiah, as the Savior, as the Redeemer, as the Healer, as the One who can make a way out of no way. Christ Jesus says, "Today, thou shalt be with Me in Paradise."

Jesus realized that this man did not have much time left. Our Lord was aware that this dying man could not wait until tomorrow, or next week, or next month, or next year—he needed a miracle right now. Today!

But before I take my seat, there may be somebody here merely looking at things as they presently are. Your sight is fixed on things the way they seem to appear. You are locked into your present set of circumstances, but if you can look at Jesus beyond what you see, beyond what you feel, and beyond what you know and walk by faith and not by sight, then you also can hear Jesus say "Today!"

Today! Sometimes I stand in need of a blessing right now. Today, sometimes I require a healer who can help me where I hurt. Today, I need a God that can save me where I suffer.

Jesus says to us, "Today, thou shall be with me in Paradise . . . where the wicked shall cease from troubling and the weary shall be at rest. Where all the saints of the ages shall sit at His feet and be blessed."

In his song "Unclouded Day," Rev. J. K. Atwood describes a beautiful vision of heaven. "O they tell me of a home far beyond the skies, O they tell me of a home far away; O they tell me of a home where no storm clouds rise, O they tell me of an unclouded day."

Are you going to be there? Are you going to be in that number when the saints go marching in? Are you going to be singing in heaven's choir? Are you going to be walking those streets of gold? Are you going to be in that place where Sabbath has no end? Today!

—Dennis East Thomas

Pastor, First African Baptist Church, Richmond, Virginia
Professor, Richmond Virginia Seminary
Regional Vice President, Lott Carey Baptist Foreign Mission Convention

"When Jesus therefore saw His mother, and the disciples whom He loved standing by, He said to His mother, 'Woman, behold your son!' Then He said to the disciple, 'Behold, your mother!'"

John 19:26–27a NKJV

CHAPTER ELEVEN

Making Provisions for Departure

Rev. Lucille L. Carrington

THE THIRD EXPRESSION FROM THE CROSS

The Gospel according to John is an excellent declaration by John who portrays the deity as the Son of God. John could not deny Luke's portrayal of the fact that this same deity is also the son of man. In this text, the human nature of the deity who is Jesus comes forth with much precision and power, much concern and compassion, much love and grace.

Here we find this same man, Jesus, hanging from the cross simply because He chose to love mankind. He has already uttered two words: one of intercession, "Father, forgive them . . ." and the other of compassion, "Today, you will be with me . . ." But, this Word, the third Word, is one of dying concern. A Word that is so unselfish until it speaks peace and comfort even when the days are few.

The operative word is "Behold." *Behold* means to look upon, to look after, or to take care of. This suggests that we have an awesome task of not only preparing for our own departure but we must also provide the necessary care for those whom we are leaving behind. Therefore, we can learn from Jesus how to make provisions for our departure.

Rev. Lucille L. Carrington

One point of interest that we should acknowledge is how Jesus speaks with such simplicity until many have missed the point. Nicodemus missed the point when Jesus said, "You must be born again" (John 3:7). The disciples missed the point when Jesus said that He must die and rise again on the third day. Many of us are still missing the point because we have yet to digest the fact that we did not come here to stay, that we are just passing through, and that we all have an unknown number of days of existence here on this earth. When we dissect this Word, we will experience some good news that will sustain and comfort those we leave here. When we allow the power of the Master to work with us and through us, the Word will open and thrust forth some provisions for our departure.

When the light of our life's lamp begins to grow dim and the excruciating pain of loss begins to reside in our loved ones, we are called upon to remind them that they are not alone because Jesus knows the pain we bear. Picture in your mind Jesus dying on the cross. He is suffering himself. He looks at those standing before Him at the cross. In the crowd, he focuses on the one woman whom God used as an instrument to bring Him into this world. The human part of Him bursts forth and He feels the pain of Mary. So, what can Jesus do? Certainly Mary must understand that what He is going through is necessary and what she is going through is also necessary.

Luke tells us in 2:23–35 that a man named Simeon had already warned Mary of the sorrow like a sharp sword that would break her heart. Suffering was going on on both sides. His torments were tortures. She was upon sorrow. He was upon the cross. Her heart bled as His body bled. But Jesus knew the pain that Mary felt. He felt a mother who had lost a son. He heard that mother's cry, "Lord, that's my son hanging on the cross." So when he looked at her, it was a look of reassurance that he feels and knows her pain.

When we lose a husband or wife; a mother or father; a boy or girl; a sister or brother; or even a best friend, the days are long and the nights are lonely. There are times when the weeds of time have grown up all around us and robbed us of our right to be free; when the sun cannot shine bright enough and the moon is in a constant state of eclipse; when the pain keeps aching and the storms keep on raging; and when the valley is dark and the mountains are too hard to climb. Remember, this pain and agony is necessary but also remember, Jesus knows where you are and He is looking right at you. This is the same look that He gave Mary saying, "I know the pain that you bear." Because He knows our pain, we can rest assured that joy will come in the morning.

We are also called upon to remind our loved ones that all of us must travel the same road from earth to glory. All of us hold different titles and positions in this world. Those titles have given us special privileges to go to high places and to have special things. Here we find Jesus having to deal with this very touching issue. Yet, the truth had to be told. If you notice, Jesus did not address Mary as His mother. He called her "Woman." Mary had to understand that Jesus did not belong to her, He belonged to God. God had used her to do special work, but the work did not give her a special status. Mary was meant to be an instrument not an icon. She was called to worship and not to be worshiped. The truth of the matter is Mary had to go through what everyone else had to go through. She had to be saved like everyone else. Mary had to travel the same road from earth to glory just like everyone else. If Jesus had called her "mother," Mary would have been looking for her special place in heaven. So, he called her "woman" instead.

Too many folks are being misled by the weight of their status. Our leaders are falling from grace because they thought that the title would buy them a license to sin. Yes, the titles before and after our names have lead many to believe that there are special places in heaven to accommodate their positions.

The apostles did not want to include Paul in their apostolic circle because he did not walk with them as they walked with Jesus. They did not understand that it takes more than physical legs to walk with the Lord. We need spiritual legs as well. The Jews thought that they would be the only ones to see heaven because they were the "chosen people." They did not understand that "chosen people" did not mean the "only people."

Jesus is not impressed by our titles, rather he is impressed by our character. There are no status positions in heaven. Whether you are a doctor, lawyer, preacher, or teacher, all of us must travel the same road from earth to glory. Unless we are caught up in the end, the songwriter said that all us have a reservation with the cemetery without the privilege of cancellation.

Finally, when we and our loved ones come to grips with the fact that Jesus knows the pain we bear and each of us must travel the same road from earth to glory, then it is time to "set our house in order." Who has Jesus placed in your care? What are you doing to provide for them? Who will hold the reins when you are gone? Once we face the reality that we did not come here to stay, we can set our house in order. To set our house in order means we must be concerned about where we are going in order to provide for how we are going. If Jesus had spoken from a selfish human perspective, he would have said, "Mama, this suffering is necessary. Mama I know the pain that you feel, but I must go to be with Daddy." This kind of language would have torn Mary apart. But Jesus did not speak in that manner. He was setting his house in order. He knew he could not give Mary what she physically needed. He had no house to put her in. The clothes on his back were taken by the Roman soldiers. He knew that Mary would not have understood if he had said, "Don't worry, I am still going to take care of you." Mary was not ready to face the fact that when God removes one comfort He raises up another one. Mary was not ready to hear any of this. Her son was leaving her all alone. What was Jesus to do? Who was going to take care of his mother?

The Bible notes that Jesus looked over and saw his "beloved disciple"—the one who Jesus loved. His name is John. Then Jesus looked at Mary again and said, "Woman, Behold your Son" (John 19:26). Jesus was saying in His heart, "Mama, I know you want me to stay with you, but I must go. But look over there. I want John to be your son. I want him to give you the earthly comfort that you need." Oh! I can see Jesus looking at John and saying, "John, I want you to take care of my mama. John, I do not have silver or gold to pay you but my Father is rich in houses and land. He holds this world in the palms of His hands. John, my Father will supply you with all you need to take care of my mama." I can hear Jesus saying, "John, sometimes the going may get tough and the hills may be hard to climb but my Father will supply you with sufficient grace to sustain you in the midst of it all."

Are you setting your house in order? There are many who are leaving here with some unfinished business. Many are acting like they came here to stay. Too many are leaving their loved ones without provisions. An alarming number of folks are walking around every day without life insurance. They do not think of the fact that someone else has to provide for their funeral expenses and their families if they leave with their houses out of order. The Lord is looking for some Johns because there are so many Marys that need to be taken care of. There are so many mamas and children that need care. There are so many souls that need to be saved.

Jesus has now made provisions for His departure. He dealt with the pain and suffering. He dealt with the truth—wanting to be free from his mother. Jesus set his house in order. Now He is ready to go home.

I wonder if you are making provisions for departure? Have you been assured as well as your loved ones that Jesus knows the pain that you bear? I am reminded of my sister. I was playing with the Lord then. I did not know Jesus but I knew about Him. I was in the military, stationed in Denver, Colorado. One day I was sitting in the mess hall eating and having fun. Someone called me and said I had a phone call. I went joyfully to the phone. On the other end was a kind voice that said, "this is the Red Cross." The bottom began to fall out of my body. Immediately I thought it was my father because he had been sick. But before I could finish my thought, the voice told me my sister has passed. My heart stopped beating. I could not see. I was lifeless. I was not ready. She was only forty-seven years old. The pain met me head on. The Red Cross rushed me home. I cried all the way. Days and months passed and I was still in pain. It was out of this experience that I really began to know who Jesus really is. I can say that even though he did not take the pain away, he knew what I was going through.

Therefore, I challenge you to get to know Jesus for yourself. You will find that he is a kind and compassionate friend. He will ease your pain, remind you of who you are, and direct you in setting your house in order.

—Lucille L. Carrington
Pastor, Morning Star Baptist Church, St. Stephens, Virginia

"Now from the sixth hour, there was darkness over all the land unto the ninth hour. And about the ninth hour, Jesus cried with a loud voice, saying 'Eli, Eli, Lama Sabachthani?' That is to say, 'My God, My God, why have you forsaken me?'"

Matthew 27:45–46 NKJV

CHAPTER TWELVE

An Anchor for Reality

Dr. E. D. McCreary Jr.

THE FOURTH EXPRESSION FROM THE CROSS

The killers of Jesus felt that crucifixion had a double meaning, a double misery. On the one hand, it meant "the anguish of a tortured body" and on the other hand, "isolation from other people." What they failed to realize is that God, the Father, shared the pain of Jesus, the Son. Hence, there was no separation between heaven and Calvary. The Son had an anchor for reality in the love of the Father for the Son.

Calvary was God's way to salvation. When Jesus died on the cross, He died as a victim, but also a victor. Matthew's Gospel clearly indicates that Jesus made a cry of delirium, "My God, My God, why hast thou forsaken me?" (Matt. 27:46 NKJV). His cry was also a cry of identification. Because He said "My God" twice in the utterance, we see a cry and an appeal to the God of our Fathers who is a Deliverer in every age.

The death of Jesus on the cross had great consequences. It must be pictured in terms of cosmic disruptions. Matthew says that "a darkness came over the land from the sixth to the ninth hour" (Matt. 27:46).

Matthew 27 says "About the ninth hour, Jesus cried with a loud voice, saying 'Eli, Eli Lama Sabachthani,' that is 'My God, My God, why have thou forsaken me?'"

A CRY OF ANGUISH

In this fourth expression from the cross, Jesus uses the faith of Israel, as given in Psalm 22:1, to bridge the gap between faith and fact. He was aware of the collision between faith and the facts of life. In that context, He makes a cry of anguish.

No doubt, Jesus knew that the psalmist had an individual lament. He knew the mood of the psalmist like the port of old; Jesus stated his sufferings in graphic terms but, like the psalmist, he was convinced of forthcoming help.

We must remember that the scriptures of Jesus were the Old Testament and that He was steeped in them. Deep down in His spirit, Jesus knew that Psalm 22 really had two parts. He knew that the first part was a cry of a troubled man, but also knew that the psalm didn't end with verse one.

The question raised by Jesus on the cross is taken from a familiar passage for every faithful servant of God. It was originally a pitiful cry of people who were oppressed by a conqueror. The tyrant had destroyed the holy places of the Hebrews and carried away many from the flower of youth into slavery.

In the Bible, Jesus is pictured as "a man of sorrows, acquainted with grief," so here is a cry of loneliness and anguish on the cross (Isa. 53:3b). In this cry, Jesus was carrying an inner cross by bearing our sins. He was the God-selected substitute for man in bearing our sins. Man's sin was His burden and the burden was heavy; hence, His cry of anguish was, "My God, My God, why have you forsaken me?"

Dr. E. D. McCreary Jr.

Every human, including Jesus, has made a cry for help at some time. At some point, we've said, as the psalmist and Jesus said earlier, "My God, My God, why have you forsaken me?" God, why are you so far from my down-sitting and uprising? Father, why are you so far from my cries of despair and my wailings of anguish?

Yes, we know what Jesus was going through when He made this fourth question, because like Him, we, too, have been objects of derision. Men have made fun of us and we have been insulted many times.

Troubles will get in our way. Troubles get up with us in the morning and troubles go to bed with us at night. Troubles go off on trips with us and troubles come back with us from these trips. As the old black slaves used to sing:

> There's trouble in the air
> There's trouble in the air
> There's trouble in the air
> There must be a God somewhere.

When troubles come, it is natural for the child of God to call on God for help. Sometimes we feel like a motherless child, abandoned by God and like Jesus, we often cry out with a loud voice saying,

> My God, My God, why have you forsaken me?
> Why are you so far from helping me
> And from the words of my groaning?
> Oh my God, I cry in the daytime
> But you do not hear me
> And in the night season
> And am not silent. (Ps. 22:1–2)

We know this cry from the logic of acquaintance.

All conscious people have a pain threshold; there's just so much we can bear. All of us get to our limit sometimes. We can only take so much. There is a point of no return for all of us. Jesus in his cry was facing the bottom of humanity with the notions of being and non-being coming to grips.

His cry was Heidegger's *Dasein*, being there for him. There was no elsewhere—*Dasein*. This is it—Calvary, the

Place of the Skull, where man's sins will be forgiven and where God's plan of salvation was worked out.

In a very real way, Jesus was saying in this fourth expression on the cross, "Look at what is happening here." This is where we are, "He is us."

A HYMN OF PRAISE AND THANKSGIVING

Psalm 22:1 that Jesus quoted on the cross is not the end of the psalm. The psalm really has two parts: the cry of anguish and a hymn of praise and thanksgiving. Jesus was, perhaps, too weak to quote the whole Psalm 22, but I believe He knew its full content. He was not only human; He was Divine. He understood paradox (two premises which at first seem to be contradictory, but both are true) because, as Soren Kierkegaard said, "Jesus is supreme paradox, very God and very man, yet one person."

Never forget that "God was in Christ, reconciling the world unto Himself" (1 Cor. 5:18). In a very special way, God was at work in Christ during the long hours when Jesus hung in agony on the cross. My theology professor at Andover Newton Theological School, Dr. Nels Ferre, described the drama of redemption in three simple, but significant sentences. He said, "God did it, God did it through Jesus Christ, God did it because He wanted to do it."

Because God, the Father, and Christ, the Son, were one, He was able to give a cry of identification saying, "*My* God, *My* God" (author's italics). Christ's God was the God of the psalmist. Both believe that:

Dominion belongs to the Lord:
He rules the nations

—Ps. 22:28

But you [God] are holy
Enthroned in the praises of Israel
Our fathers trusted in you, and were delivered.
You made me trust while on my mother's breast
You have been my God

—Ps. 22:3–4, 9

O my strength, hasten to help me
Save me from the lion's mouth.
You have answered me and I will declare your name to my brethren

—Ps. 22:19–21, 22

AN ANCHOR FOR REALITY

That's why in the end, He could say, "It is finished" and "Father into your hands I commend my spirit" (the sixth and seventh expressions from the cross) (John 19:30). Here was a certainty of God's great Love.

May I conclude by saying that when you are really in atonement with God in Christ, when you review God's goodness to us, especially in times of trouble, we too, like our Lord, will have an anchor for reality.

My brothers and sisters, the fourth expression from the cross is not the last one. Stay to the end of this service and hear my partner in the ministry, the Reverend Dr. Earl Brown, explain the last prayer, "Father, into Thy hands, I commend my spirit."

The cross-resurrection experience is a hyphenated phenomenon. Good Friday is really meaningless without Easter and vice versa. We cannot have one without the other. Earth's blackest day is just a few days apart from earth's brightest day. Good Friday and Easter go together.

On this blessed day, we glory in the cross which towers over the wrecks of time and on Easter Sunday, we glory in the resurrection of our Lord. Easter Sunday is resurrection time, a time to proclaim that Jesus Christ is alive and well.

The crucified and resurrected Christ is our Lord and Master. When anyone has an encounter with the Living Lord, that person can sing:

My soul is anchored in the Lord,
In the Lord, In the Lord,
My soul is anchored in the Lord.
Amen and Amen.

—E. D. McCreary Jr.
Pastor Emeritus, Mount Carmel Baptist Church
Professor Emeritus, Virginia Union University

"After this, Jesus knowing that all things were now accomplished, that the scripture might be fulfilled, saith, I thirst. Now there was set a vessel full of vinegar: and they filled a sponge with vinegar and put it upon hyssop, and put it to his mouth."

John 19:28–29

CHAPTER THIRTEEN

I Thirst

Dr. Robert E. Williams Sr.

THE FIFTH EXPRESSION FROM THE CROSS

This fifth saying of Jesus on the cross has its unique reporting through the Johannine account of the crucifixion. It marks the first mention by Jesus of anything that might be construed as a reference to his physical condition. Until now his primary focus has been on others. There is, however, less evidence in his utterance of a spiritual, non-physical dimension. Recalling the preaching/teaching style of this master of "Earthly messages with heavenly meanings" yields unto us divine, even prophetic, implications in the expression, "I thirst."

UNDERSTANDING JESUS THE PREACHER/TEACHER

Those who heard and followed Him often misunderstood Jesus. He frequently spoke in terms which were misconstrued by even his closest followers, the disciples. Leonardo da Vinci once said, "Nothing can be loved or hated unless it is first known."

When Jesus got the news that Lazarus was sick, he immediately announced, ". . . this sickness is not unto death . . ." (John 11:4). He told His disciples ". . . Our friend Lazarus

Dr. Robert E. Williams Sr.

sleepeth; but I go that I may awake him out of sleep." The disciples replied, "Lord, if he sleep, he shall do well" (John 11:11–12). These men did not understand how Jesus used words. They thought he meant Lazarus was taking a sleep of rest. So He said to them plainly, ". . . Lazarus is dead" (John 11:13–14).

Even as a child, Jesus uttered sayings not clear to the natural minded. At age twelve, he could not be found by his parents for three days during a family journey to Jerusalem for the high holy days. When he was found, they were amazed that he was in the temple in the midst of doctors, both listening to and asking them questions. His mother said unto him, "Son, why hast thou thus dealt with us? . . . thy father and I have sought for thee sorrowing." He said unto them, "How is it that you sought me? Wist ye not that I must be about my Father's business?" (Luke 2:49). Though they were his parents, they did not understand the meaning of his words. Joseph, his earthly father knew that he had not sent his twelve-year-old son out on any business.

Once Jesus told religious leaders ". . . Destroy this temple and in three days I will raise it up." They thought he was referring to the natural temple. He was speaking of his body (John 2:19–21).

On another occasion while Jesus was teaching in a house, a messenger came and said, "Your mother and your brothers are outside desiring to speak with you." He answered and said, "Who is my mother and who are my brethren?" Then with his hands stretched toward his disciples he said, "Behold my mother and my brethren!" Here Jesus changed the basis of their relationship to him. He said, ". . . Whosoever shall do the will of my Father, which is in heaven, the same is my brother and sister and mother" (Matt. 12:46–50).

Although many common phrases became idiomatic when they fell from the lips of Jesus, they always had a literal sense in application. Rather than saying, "I'm making a spiritual use of everyday earthly words," Jesus simply spoke them as if everyone was supposed to understand the spiritual meaning. He sought to convert and train men to grasp the spiritual meaning of words used in carnal, earthly expressions. Hence, he says to an old man, a master in Israel, "You must be born again," not from your mother's womb, not by human procreative process, but from above (John 3:3–7). Alas! He imparts to us that which not only yields new birth, but that which opens the gateway to a better understanding of him. He gives us faith to believe God. Kahlil Gibran said in his masterpiece *The Prophet*: ". . . .the teacher who walks in the shadow of the temple, among his followers gives not of his wisdom, but rather of his faith and lovingness." Therefore, the faith we embrace is, "Not of ourselves it is the gift of God through Jesus Christ" (Eph. 2:8).

WHEN JESUS SPEAKS OF THIRST

There were at least three occasions prior to the cross when Jesus spoke of thirst. Consider his meaning and purpose in these instances. First, note the encounter with the woman at the well. She had a thirst within her soul that had never been quenched. Jesus knew that her greatest need was not filling the water bucket she brought to the well. So he gave her water that satisfies the thirsty soul, that which springs up unto everlasting life (John 1:14). He invested in her the well of salvation.

Second, once while in Jerusalem, Jesus stood and cried, "If any man thirst let him come unto me and drink." This was not an invitation to receive natural water; He declared, "He that believeth on me, as the Scripture hath said, out of his belly shall flow rivers of living water." This was a promise of the Holy Spirit to all that believe in him (John 7:38–39).

Finally, in the Sermon on the Mount, Jesus taught, "Blessed are they which do hunger and thirst after righteousness sake; for theirs is the kingdom of heaven" (Matt. 5:6). To thirst after righteousness sake is to thirst after right standing with God. This relationship level with God is accomplished not by what one does, but by what one believes. The Scripture record says, ". . . Abraham believed God, and it was counted unto him for righteousness." Therefore, it is belief rather than behavior that makes one right with God. Belief promotes a thirst for more. Jesus said this kind of thirst shall be filled. Such belief drives behavior that pleases God. This kind of thirsty soul places the Lord at the apex of life's priorities.

JESUS SAYS, "I THIRST"

Here it is noteworthy to consider not only what Jesus said, but when and why He said it. John 19:28–29 states ". . . After this!" After he forgave his executioners, After this! After he hindered death to make one more reservation in paradise, After this! After he made possible through John an adoption to guarantee the care of His widowed mother, After this! After having known no sin but becoming sin for us, He discovered the Father's back was turned on him!

After this, he knew that he had become the fulfillment of the Old Testament taboo, ". . . He that is hanged (from a tree) is accursed of God" (Deut. 21:23). Yet, in this, though he was cut off by the law, he was also made free from the law, since those who died such a death were considered outcast and no longer within its sphere. The law now has been nailed to the cross with Jesus, done away with. There is now a new and living way to God i.e., through Jesus who is the Christ.

Now Jesus knows that the sum total of his mission as the Vicarious Atonement is complete. There is but one more Scripture from the Old Testament to fulfill on this cross. Six hours before when they brought him to Golgotha, they offered him wine mingled with myrrh (painkiller). They wanted to stupefy him; he wanted to go through with a clear mind. He wanted to endure the cross, despising the shame.

Now six hours later he says, "I thirst!" Well, what's the matter with Jesus? I'll tell you what it is. This is the same Jesus who said, ". . . Lo, I come (in the volume of the book, it is written of me) to do thy will, O God" (Heb. 10:7). Now it's time to get ready to go! But he still remembers one more Scripture. He now recalls another word from the Lord that says, "they gave me gall for my meat, and in my thirst they gave me vinegar to drink" (Ps. 69:21).

After six hours on the cross, he must have been thirsty in his natural body, scorching with fever from inflammation of the wounds he bore. Still, more than his natural body, his soul thirsted for righteousness. They thought he wanted relief for parched lips. They thought his pleas desired an ease from the pain. But the Bible declares he cried out that the Scripture might be fulfilled. Now we know the reason he cried out because the Word tells us why. When they heard him say "I thirst," one man on the ground ran to him with a sponge tied to the end of a hyssop reed, dipped in sour wine. He raised it up to his mouth. His cry caused the word spoken by the psalmist David to be fulfilled.

Jesus fought a good fight. Jesus got the victory over his course. Yes, with a body battered and torn he did not have much left to work with. Look at him!

Caught up between earth and glory
Tormented between God and man;
Isolated while hanging between two thieves;
Humiliated with his breath almost gone!

As Theodore Roosevelt once said, "Do what you can, with what you have, where you are."

Now wouldn't it be good if every child of God would rise up and say, "Lord, I made up my mind. I'm gonna do what I can with whatever you gave me! And I'll do it right here where I am!"

I Thirst

If I can thirst for righteousness like Jesus did, then I know I shall be filled. Some glad morning I will be able to sing with Isaac Watts:

When I can read my title clear,
To mansions in the skies
I'll bid farewell to every fear
And wipe my weeping eyes.

Should earth against my soul engage
And fiery darts be hurled
Then I can smile at Satan's rage
And face a frowning world.

—from *Training in Christianity*, translated by Walter Lowie, pp. 66–70.

—Robert E. Williams Sr.
Pastor, Christian Tabernacle Baptist Church
Instructor, Richmond Virginia Seminary

"When Jesus therefore had received the vinegar, He said, 'It is finished'; and He bowed His head and gave up the ghost."

John 19:30

CHAPTER FOURTEEN

A Done Deal

Dr. Clifton Whitaker Jr.

THE SIXTH EXPRESSION FROM THE CROSS

Having been called to preach on June 2, 1979, and after sharing this with my dad whom I considered one of the greatest preachers in the world, he said "Son, you must go to school!" After two years of undergraduate education and three years of seminary at the School of Religion, Virginia Union University, I finished. It was a done deal. At graduation, I observed my dad crying. He said, "Son, I'm crying because it's all over, you've finished, it's a done deal and I can die happy and proud of your accomplishment."

In this text, we are focusing on the Sixth Expression coming from the lips of Jesus while hanging on the cross on Calvary's hill. One of the finest things in life is when we have finished an assignment, especially when that assignment brings feelings of accomplishment, excitement, joy, and jubilation. The word "finished" is the same as "paid-in-full." Jesus came to finish God's work of Salvation, to pay in full the penalty for our sins. It's Friday afternoon in Jerusalem, and the sun has already gone down behind the western hills because Jesus is dying.

The only begotten Son of God is in the process of being through with His earthly mission. I can imagine that there's a sense of accomplishment, excitement, joy, and jubilation because He's finally arrived at the point of a done deal. He said, "It is finished!" He is being crucified for your sins and mine. He could have come down but he decided to stay there. He could have summoned ten thousand angels to rescue Him from this humiliating ordeal but He didn't. O yes, he could have said, "Father, I've changed my mind," but He didn't. He realized why He was born and why He had been sent into the world. He came in order for us to have life and have it abundantly.

It was a Divine Assignment! He was sent here by His Heavenly Father as John 3:16 reminds us, "For God so loved the world that He gave His only begotten Son, that whosoever believeth in Him should not perish, but have everlasting life." So the bottom line is that it was a deal or an arrangement, a Covenant between God and His son on behalf of all mankind.

Also it was understood that the deal required Jesus to die for the remission and forgiveness of our sins. After His death, we would freely be able to approach God for ourselves and have a right to the Tree of Life. Having lived among mankind for thirty-three years, I can imagine He probably had some reservations about giving up His life. As a matter of fact, while in the Garden of Gethsemene, He fell on His knees and His human side prayed, "O my Father, if it be possible, let this cup pass from me." However, His Divine side prayed, "Nevertheless, not as I will but as thou wilt" (Matt. 26:39). The Master was expressing the fact that He was both human and divine, fully man and fully God.

In spite of all that was happening to Him and around Him, He never forgot the agreement, the deal, and reason He came to earth in the first place. With all of the good He had performed, He never took credit for Himself, always giving credit and praise to His Father. That's one of the main problems in life, we are so quick to take credit for ourselves, even though without God we can do nothing. We can't do anything by ourselves.

Dr. Clifton Whitaker Jr.

Like Paul and Apollos, we can plant it and water it, but it is God who gives the increase. It is God who can make a way when there appears to be no way. When the troubles of the world have burdened us down, it is God who is our present help in a time of trouble. It is this same God, who allowed His only Begotten Son to suffer, bleed, and die on that Old Rugged Cross. The record is, just before Jesus died, before He completed the deal, before He finished His assignment and gave up the Ghost,

He uttered three of the most powerful words in the universe, "It is finished." No doubt, He was speaking to His Father when He said, "It is finished." Father, it is a done deal, I've completed my assignment. It reminds me of the words from Paul, the Apostle, at the close of his ministry. When he realized that his life was about to come to an end, he said, "I've finished my course." Oh yes, Jesus, the son of God, finished His course. He closed the chapter. He completed the mandate which had been assigned to His hands. The deal was consummated and terminated.

"Father! My Father! I've done all that I can do. I've been beaten, ridiculed, spat on, tortured with a crown of seventy-two thorns pressed upon my head, speared in my side, and called everything except your child. But Father, it's all over now. It's a done deal! I have reached the comma of my life, and now I'm ready to come home.

"Just a few days ago, while sitting in the guest chamber of the upper room, serving bread and wine, I told my disciples that I was going away to prepare a place for them. I told them that I would come again and receive them unto myself so that where I am they would be also.

"Now, that I've fulfilled my promise to you, I want to keep my promise to them. 'It is finished and I'm ready to come home.' Yes, I realize that I came to seek and save that which was lost, and I did the best that I could. But now, it's a done deal, and it's all over. I have fulfilled my mission. I've completed my assignment that has been laid at my hand; now I'm ready to sit at your right hand and make intercession for those who are willing to deny themselves, to pick up the cross and follow me."

As we prepare to bring this message to closure, I think about the goodness of Jesus and all He's done for me. I think about how He gave His life, way back on Calvary, by declaring, "It's finished." Therefore, I would like to borrow those prophetic words from Thomas Shepherd, when he said,

Must Jesus Bear the cross alone
And all the world go free?
No, there's a cross for every one
And there's a cross for me.

The Consecrated cross I'll bear
Till death shall set me free,
And then go home my crown to wear,
For there's a crown for me. It is a Done Deal.

—Clifton Whitaker Jr.
Pastor, Grayland Baptist Church, Richmond, Virginia
Academic Dean of the School of Religion, Richmond Virginia Seminary

"When Jesus had received the vinegar, he said, "It is finished" and he bowed his head and gave up his spirit."

John 19:30 NIV

CHAPTER FIFTEEN

It Is Finished

Dr. Earl Brown

THE SEVENTH EXPRESSION FROM THE CROSS

The pains, struggles, problems, and purpose of Jesus' life fell from His lips while he suffered on the cross. We often try to remember a person's last words whether it's a mother, father, or some other relative or close friend. His or her last words linger with us for years. The last words of Christ have lingered with us for nearly two thousand years.

We hear Him cry out "It is finished." Yet, these words were also words of triumph and victory. Jesus knew the comfort which is to be found in God during the time He faced death. He knew the comfort of God's presence and blessings, and He reveals it.

Jesus was about to die when He uttered these last words. Jesus endured and suffered death as wages, the punitive transgressions. He removed death's sting and robbed death of its victory because He was dying for us.

Jesus had already died many times inwardly as he observed us sinning; therefore, the cross was just a final nail in the coffin.

There was also hope for a better day in His dying that senses He was dying for us. There would be forgiveness of our sins. His dying made it more comfortable for us to die because if we die in Him, we will have eternal life with Him.

His death was not the end because there would be a resurrection: "From that time forth began Jesus to show unto His disciples, how that He must go into Jerusalem, and suffer . . . . and be killed, and be raised again the third day" (Matt. 16:21).

The believers of Jesus can be comforted by His last words, having been given another chance. When troubled by sin, burdens, or sorrows, resurrection is there to remind us that "It is finished" may have been His last words, but not His last experience with us.

In these last words, great love is shown. For the cross shows us this greatness of the love of God. In Romans 5:8, we are shown the beauty of God's love for sinners. The only way to discover His love for us is by coming to the cross. At the cross, God meets us in love. Jesus had said that God is love, but it was on the cross that these words took fire: "For God so loved the world that He gave His only begotten Son . . ." (John 3:16). Every generation finds the words "It is finished" to be its accuser, its means of salvation.

We can understand Jesus' victory through the words "It is finished." In earthly terms, His death is not a sign of God's majesty and power but an unforgettable reminder of the lengths to which He will go to bring us to Him. As great and powerful as symbols can be, the cross was more than a symbol; it was an action. Jesus did something which achieves what God alone can do. He bore the shame of our sins, our rebellion, and our failure. In the cross, He made vivid and available to us forgiveness, redemption, and release. Moreover, what He did in that intimate identification with humanity in its sin and sorrow, he still does.

For this cause we have hope, we have confidence, we have assurance "It is finished" because this divine Christ takes away the sins of the world by His union with every sinner who, by faith, will receive Him. We are not deserted.

We can understand our salvation because "It is finished." Through the cross, Jesus has given us His earnest concern to save us from sin and death. This is not just one philosophy of life

Dr. Earl Brown

among many others. This is the gospel; this is the good news.

Although the cross always reminds us of Jesus' death, the philosophy of the cross is a philosophy of life. "It is finished" is life through death. It is finding a new way of life by rejecting the ways of self-love, self-trust, and self-assertion. Our salvation, our peace, and our fulfillment of God's purpose for us begins with our acceptance of He who died for us. Salvation is of God alone.

As Paul puts it, "All things are of God, who hath reconciled us to himself by Jesus Christ" (2 Cor. 5:18). Salvation is not anything we can do; it is what God has done for us through the cross. God will give this gift to anyone who believes, to anyone who puts their trust in the crucified Christ.

In conclusion, Christ said "It is finished" because under the circumstances of that time, it was inevitable that He would die. Likewise, it has been inevitable that John the Baptist and other martyrs should die not only because tyrants now govern the nations, but because men are what they are. "It is impossible that a prophet should perish away from Jerusalem" (Luke 13:33).

"It is finished" because in this world, which always destroys its best, the political, social, and religious conditions always continue to make Christ a martyr and lead to the murder of the prophet.

"It is finished" because it was so written in Isaiah 53, Psalm 22, and elsewhere that the scriptures themselves reflect and in a measure interpret this fatal trait in human nature and in the world's history.

"It is finished" because God permitted it and because God is absolutely sovereign. He must will what he permits. God's purpose is evident from the later consequences, the removal of sin, the breakdown of barriers between the self and the world, the whole new life in grace, the creation, and the new being in Christ.

"It is finished" because He himself willed to die by taking the risk involved in going to Jerusalem, of which anyone could have warned Him. This was the acceptance of God's way for Him to go. Out of it came and continue to come the blessings of a new life, taken for all who accept His way, take up His cross, and live in Him.

—Earl Brown

Pastor, Fifth Baptist Church, Richmond, Virginia
President of the Baptist General Convention of Virginia

CHAPTER SIXTEEN

Dealing With Your Adversaries

Every leader soon discovers that there are persons with whom he or she is working very closely who are not in agreement with him or her. All of us know some persons who claim to be with us, yet they are not. Many of these persons shake your hand with a smile on their faces while, for reasons beyond your control, they are often found opposing the things that you are trying to foster.

In my ministry, my attention has been called and I have observed that despite my plans, there are always these negative voters. My friends have given me some advice on how I can get rid of them. Yet, I have permitted it to go on for long periods of time. I have learned during these fifty years in the Gospel Ministry there is great value in not moving too quickly. For me, the waiting period gives me two things: first, it gives me the opportunity to become aware if he or she has a personal dislike for me; secondly, it also gives this person an opportunity to understand me better. If it means accepting a few negative statements to end up finally with a supporter, then the wait and the discomfort will be worth it.

So many times, some of my closest friends have asked me, "Benjamin, why do you continue, knowing that a person is against you, to act as if you are not aware of what's happening?" In my fifty years in the Gospel Ministry, I have been able to accomplish more by permitting the antagonistic person to go far enough for others to see what he or she is trying to do. The more persons who see that this individual is working against their leader will give the leader more support if he or she ever wanted to remove that person.

Sometimes a leader moves immediately to get rid of an individual whom he or she really believes is working against the program. When he or she moves before the other members of the organization have seen this opposition, it leaves the leader in a position as if he or she is picking on or just dislikes this person. Then this person gains the sympathy of the body. From that moment on, this person will be shielded against any attention in which the leader attempts to show his deliberate opposition.

We usually make very few recommendations to our Administrative Board. Yet, I know before the recommendations are read that there are those who would ask unnecessary questions. Once all questions have been answered, I am also aware of the person who would vote against the recommendations.

Remember that "the Lord Jesus himself said, 'It is more blessed to give than to receive.'"

Acts 20:35 NIV

CHAPTER SEVENTEEN

To Receive Is Good, to Give Is Better

Dr. Joseph B. Underwood

The apostle Paul, with his Holy Spirit–inspired insights (cf. 1 Cor. 2), rescued from oblivion a Beatitude spoken by Jesus, but proclaimed by Paul alone: "It is more blessed to give than to receive" (Acts 20:35 NIV).

The Bible is filled with many Beatitudes. Jesus initiated his "Sermon on the Mount" with a series of Beatitudes, reminding us of God's intense desire for our true blessedness. God is so concerned that we be filled with overflowing joy that issues from those qualities of character that are inherent in the being of God Himself, that he gave Himself in Christ that we might share His blessedness—life abundant!

Jesus taught that the way to find life is to give one's self away. "Whoever wants to save his life will lose it, but whoever loses his life for me will find it" (Matt. 16:25 NIV). "Unless a kernel of wheat falls into the ground and dies, it remains only a single seed. But if it dies it produces many seeds. The man who loves his life will lose it, while the man who hates his life in this world will keep it for eternal life" (John 12:24-25 NIV).

Thus does Jesus reverse the world's standard of values. Jesus says, "The way to get up is by getting down. The way to live is by dying to self. The way to be first is by being servant of all. The way to find happiness is to give! As C. B. Williams translates this Beatitude: "It makes one happier to give than to get!" In other words: Although it is good to receive, giving is better!

One writer called this saying of Jesus, "The Supreme Beatitude," because it reveals God's motive both in creation and in redemption.

"God is love" (1 John 4:10). But love cannot exist in a vacuum. Love cannot exist between a person and things. Love exists only between persons. God is love—so God created man, that He might have a person to love and a person to reciprocate love. How do we know what love is? asks John, and answers: "By the fact that Jesus Christ gave his life for us" (cf. 1 John 3:16). And this, says the apostle, means that we must give ourselves for others (v. 17).

In other words, LOVE is spelled G-I-V-E!

For that is the nature of love: to give and give and give to the beloved. And true love is never satisfied by giving the cheap, the tawdry, the costless. Love gives that which costs—and costs dearly! "For God so loved the world, that He gave His only begotten Son, that whosoever believes in Him, should not perish, but have eternal life" (John 3:16). That is why it is happier to give than to receive: because love, if real, is characterized by the unquenchable urge to give to the one who is loved.

So, when sin separated man from God, causing man to spurn God's giving of himself to man, God, because He is love, kept on giving—even to the cross! The cross is the measure of God's love for us, of God's desire to give us *Himself*! When we receive this gift, God Himself, then we experience life that *is* life! This is the primary reason why "it is more blessed to give than to receive": *Giving is Godlike; Getting is animal-like.*

For example, you and I inhale the fresh air, retaining oxygen but exhaling carbon-dioxide. Trees and vegetables do the opposite.

Dr. Joseph B. Underwood

Have you or I ever said, "Let's get busy and exhale carbon-dioxide so as to benefit the forests?" Do the forests exhale oxygen in order to help us human beings? Of course not. We exhale the carbon-dioxide because to retain it would poison us. The trees exhale the oxygen because to retain it would be self-destructive. When, in our living of life, we give only that which we do not need, we stoop to the level of the animal or vegetable. When, however, we give that which we need in order that others may be blessed, even at great cost to ourselves, we are getting up on the God-level of life, for "God proves His love for us, in that while we were yet sinners, Christ died for us" (Romans 5:8). "This is the way God's love has been shown, namely, God sent His only Son into the world, that we through Him might have life. In this way is seen true love, not that we loved God but that He loved us and sent His Son to be the atoning sacrifice for our sins" (1 John 4:9-10 WILLIAMS).

When we give that which really costs us something, then, and only then, are we beginning to get close to God's kind of giving. And that is when we experience the reality of true blessedness and abiding joy. We then know, from experience, that it is more blessed to give than to receive! That, "To give is happier than to get!"

Jesus, however, surprises us with other reasons why "it is more blessed to give." In fact, if you will read carefully the first three Gospels to see what Jesus says about money, earning and using it, you will discover several surprises, even a few shocks!

You will probably be shocked to discover that Jesus said more about money and its correct use than he said about any other one subject. On an average, one out of each seven or eight verses in those three Gospels concerns the right use of money. Don't you suppose that's because money tends to become God's chief rival in our hearts and pursuits? Money is necessary, and the things money can buy become so alluring that we easily become much more preoccupied with its acquisition and accumulation than we do about God Himself. Jesus taught, "Seek first the kingdom of God and His righteousness" (Matthew 6:33).

Jesus, after urging us to trust the heavenly Father to supply our basic needs, reminding us that anxious worrying cannot add a hair to our head nor a minute to our life span, and assuring us of the Father's great care, says: "As your first duty, keep on looking for His standard of doing right, and for His will." Then, after that essential emphasis, he adds: If you do so, "all these things" (food, clothing, shelter) "will be added unto you" (Matthew 6:33 WILLIAMS).

It is in introducing this admonition not to worry that Jesus shocks us with a surprising reason for its being "more blessed to give than to receive." Listen:

> Do not store up for yourselves treasures on earth, where moth and rust destroy, and where thieves break in and steal. But store up for yourselves treasures in heaven, where moth and rust do not destroy, and where thieves do not break in and steal. For where your treasure is, there your heart will be also (Matthew 6:19-21 NIV).

Store up treasures in heaven. Why? Because they are safe there! Giving to God is the only way to make a safe and permanent investment! Stock markets crash, banks fail, trustees steal, inflation robs you of your treasure's value, the elements erode and destroy. What you give to God is eternally secure!

A gentleman was visiting a friend whose fortune had been destroyed overnight by the Great Depression. He looked out the window to a familiar church building and remembered that his friend, now utterly devastated economically, had given a million dollars to that church, for its building and ministries. The visitor inquired of his bankrupt friend: "Don't you wish you had kept the money you threw way, giving to that church?" "Absolutely not!" exclaimed the man. "That's the only money I saved!" he added. "Everything I kept and all I invested in other areas is gone, gone forever. All the money I gave to God will go on bearing fruit for God and for the blessing of humanity until Jesus comes again."

What you give to God and for God's use is permanently secure. Moreover, it gains at a fabulous rate of interest! When Jesus said to the rich young ruler, "Go, sell what you have, give to the poor, and you will have treasures in heaven; then, come, follow me," the man went away, unwilling to sacrifice his wealth in order to experience God. As the man, sorrowfully but fatally, departed, Jesus exclaimed to His disciples, "How hard is it for the rich to enter the kingdom of God" (cf. Mark 10:17-32). Whereupon, his disciples inquired: "Lord, we have left all to follow you, what are we going to get?" (paraphrased).

Jesus did not rebuke Peter and the others for the question. Rather, he said: "No one who has left home or brothers, or sisters or mothers or fathers or children or fields for me and the gospel will fail to receive a hundred times as much in this present age . . . and in the age to come, eternal life" (see Mark 10:24–31). How much interest is "a hundred times as much"? No, not 100 percent; 10,000 percent! Where else can you gain that kind of interest?

Give says Jesus, for I want to make you rich—rich in spiritual wealth, rich in brothers and sisters, parents and children, opportunities and fruit of all kind, rich in wealth that will glorify God and bless you and the world around you forever! And remember: it is eternally secure!

A third reason Jesus gives for why "it is more blessed to give than to receive" is found in Luke 6:38: "Give, and it will be given to you. A good measure, pressed down, shaken together and running over, will be poured into your lap." Into your bosom, it should read, for that is the place of the real gain—in your heart, mind, soul, attitudes, conduct. The real place of the gain is *you*! In your heart and soul!

Read the context: Luke 6:27-36. Jesus is saying: "Give love to your enemies, not hate; give blessing to those who curse you; give prayer for those who mistreat and abuse you; give the other cheek to those who insult you; give help to those in need; give TLC to the hurting and do unto others as you would want them to do unto you . . ." Then your reward will be great, and you will be sons of the Most High, because He is kind to the ungrateful and wicked. Be merciful, just as your Father is merciful. (Paraphrase)

It is concerning all this that Jesus urges: "Give, and it will be given unto you, super-abundantly into your real self!" If you give all of this you will be so like your heavenly Father that men will see your good works, and your likeness to Jesus, and they will glorify our Father who is in heaven. And that's the greatest blessedness you can possibly experience! Paul reminds us that in creating us "anew in Christ Jesus" it is God's intention that we "be like God in true righteousness and holiness" (Eph. 4:24 NIV).

A father had the heartbreaking task of telling his young son that his illness was fatal and he would soon die. He added quickly, "But, you are not afraid to die, are you? Daddy's little man is a Christian and he's not afraid to die, is he?" The boy squeezed the tears from his eyes, and said: "No, daddy, I'm not afraid to die; daddy, if God is like you, I'm not afraid to die!" That is the supreme wealth with which God can bless us—to make us like unto himself! That's the blessedness of giving as God gives!

A fourth reason why "it is more blessed (happier) to give than to get" is that *by giving to God, that part of us which has been reduced to the material can be transformed into redeemed personality!* What is money? Money is "coined personality." We spend our strength and days, our intelligence and talents, our skills and muscles in many hours of labor. And that part of us is gone forever. All we have to show for it is the piece of material—be it silver or paper—that we receive for spending that part of ourselves in labor.

To me, it is horribly sad that a part of me, a part of my person, has been turned into the material. I want to know: Is there any way by which I can transform that "coined personality" back into living, redeemed, and redemptive personality?

Yes, yes! There is a way. I can bring that "coined personality" and give it to God, for Him to use it in proclaiming the gospel, and in many kinds of Christian ministries for the blessing and redemption of others. As they come to know Christ, that part of me that had been reduced to coin is now transformed into redeemed persons who glorify God and bless their fellow man.

How wonderful! How marvelous! That material to which a part of me was reduced can be transformed into men and women, youth and children who are living, no longer the captives of satan, but as redeemed persons who by their lives and witness are telling others how to find new life in Jesus Christ!

One of the happiest persons and families I have known was a doctor-surgeon from Memphis, Tennessee, who left a medical practice that netted him $100,000 per year to go as a medical missionary, with a total income of approximately $3,000 per year. He went first to one of the neediest countries of Asia and then to another, equally needy, in East Africa. It was my privilege, during the nearly thirty years he served as a missionary, to visit him in three countries and see firsthand some of the blessed results, medical and evangelistic. He and his family served several years in India, when our only means of entry into that country of approximately one billion people was through a medical ministry.

For a while the house in which the family resided was also the clinic in which his medical ministry was also centered. I shall never forget the morning, just as we finished breakfast, when he said to me: "We already have a hundred people in the yard and on the verandah of the house, waiting for medical attention. Before the nurses and I begin our services, we would like for you to bring a message about Christ and salvation." During the next ten minutes the Holy Spirit gave me a message from the New Testament to share with those men and women who so desperately needed Christ and *life,* as well as health! The Spirit of God worked miraculously in their hearts, as only He can!

As I saw their spiritual hunger and receptivity to the message of Christ, I thanked God for those medical missionaries, who gave themselves to the mission to which God led them, without complaint about giving up a fortune in money, and I thanked God for the people at home who believed as did that family, that it is more blessed to give than to get, and therefore, had given generously, even sacrificially, that the message of God's redemptive love and power could be made known to those who hitherto lived in spiritual darkness and death.

I saw that day, and its verification on a return visit, the material transformed into redeemed lives and personalities and praised God for those who had experienced the blessedness of giving that God might be glorified and a part of the world redeemed.

From what I have seen in redeemed personalities in more than one hundred nations of the world I can testify, yes, I know:

It is more blessed to give than to receive!

—Joseph B. Underwood

One of the sons of Cedar Street Baptist Church of God
Missionary for the Southern Baptist Convention prior to coming to Richmond and uniting with this church.

Dr. Darrel Rollins

"I love the Lord, for He heard my voice: He heard my cry for mercy."
Psalms 116:1

CHAPTER EIGHTEEN

The Lord Has Been Good to Me

Dr. Darrel Rollins

There is something about Psalm 116 that resonates with my spirit. If I were to divide this Psalm up into sections, I would call the first section "God is Good." The psalmist highlights the fact that God is good; first, because God hears and answers prayer. "I love the Lord, for He heard my voice: He heard my cry for mercy" (Ps. 116:1). I don't know about anybody else, but I'm glad I serve a God who hears and answers prayer. Sometimes as we journey through life, we may feel that there's nobody who understands, nobody who knows, or nobody who even cares. But here the psalmist reminds us that we are never alone. We have a God who not only cares but who hears and responds to our calls for help. Therefore, the psalmist says, "I will call on the Lord as long as I live" (116:2).

If you know that somebody's listening, then you'll keep on talking. Since we know that God is listening, we would be fools not to keep on talking. That is why Jesus said, "Men ought always to pray and not to faint." Paul said "We should pray without ceasing" (Luke 18:1). Alfred Lloyd Tennyson said, "More things are wrought through prayer than this world dreams of." God hears and he answers prayer. God is good because he is a God who responds to our deepest needs. He hears the groaning and unuttered moaning of our spirits. As soon as we groan, God hears. When we soak our pillows at night with solitary tears, God hears each teardrop as it falls onto our pillows. God hears and he answers prayer.

The psalmist obviously had gone through some near death experience, and he personifies death as being the enemy. In verses three through six, he says:

> The cords of death entangled me, the anguish of the grave came upon me. I was overcome with trouble and sorrow, then I called on the name of the Lord. Oh Lord, save me. God, He says, is gracious and righteous. Our God is full of compassion. The Lord protects the simple hearted. When I was in great need, the Lord saved me. God is good because he protects and saves.

Our God is a God who is righteous. He has righteous standards and righteous expectations for us. None of us really lives up to God's expectations for us. None of us fulfills our potential that God has ordained for our lives; yet, in spite of our shortcomings and the fact that we are not what we should be, God still hears and God still responds.

God also protects us (Ps. 116:6). The world is full of trouble and danger. Some of it we bring on ourselves by our foolish behavior. Yet, our God is so loving and good that he protects us from trouble. He saves us from trouble. God is a God who saves to the uttermost. He has compassion. He has righteous stands, but our God is compassionate; in spite of ourselves, he loves us, protects us, and saves us.

The psalmist was so overwhelmed when he thought about how God had delivered him, how God had loved him, and how God had compassion on him that he begins to talk to himself in verse 7. At first he's addressing others. Then, when he gets down to verse 7, he breaks off and begins talking to himself.

Sometimes we need to talk to ourselves. Some of us won't let anybody else talk to us so at least we ought to talk to ourselves. We ought to rehearse for ourselves the goodness of God. In verse 7, he says, "be at rest once more, O my soul, for the Lord has been good to you." I'm certain that each of us can say, like the psalmist, "God has been good to me." If we spend more time thinking about how good the Lord is to us and praising God for his blessing in our lives, life would be more full of joy. We would be a lot happier if we would reflect and concentrate on the goodness of God—how God saves, protects, and delivers us.

After talking to himself, he then begins to talk to God (Ps. 116:8). "For you, Oh Lord, have delivered my soul from death. My eyes from tears, my feet from stumbling, that I may walk before the Lord in the land of the living. I believe, therefore I said, I am greatly afflicted; and in my dismay I said all men are liars." The first point I made is God is good. The second point is a strange one: there is value in distress. It is in distress that you really discover how good God is. When you go through life and it's smooth sailing with the wind at your back, it's easy to take that blessing for granted. But when times get hard and you find yourself in difficult situations; when you come to the edge of the grave and you call upon the Lord to deliver you, you'll find out just how good God really is. It's in distress that you learn to exercise faith. If everything is going right, your temptation is to trust yourself. When everything is going right, you take things for granted. When you find yourself in distressful situations that are beyond your physical limitations, it is then that you come to know that there is a God who has power that transcends all human limitations. Then you find out that "man's extremity is God's opportunity." It's in distress that we are forced to exercise our faith. For instance, think of what happens to a muscle that doesn't get any exercise: it atrophies and becomes weak. However, when you exercise that muscle it becomes strong. Distress gives us the opportunity to exercise faith. When we exercise our faith, our faith becomes stronger. So there is value in distress.

The value of distress is that we come to learn that there is a God who has all power and is all sufficient. The value is that we learn not to depend only upon human solutions. The value is that we come to understand the vanity of humanity and the arrogance of human systems and structures, which are designed to turn us away from God. Mankind with all of our technological achievements has gotten to the point where we have become so arrogant and full of vanity that we believe that all of this is simply the result of our own genius, completely discrediting the God factor. We recognize our own achievements instead of recognizing that all knowledge comes from God; thus, we choose to take credit for ourselves. The psalmist has an answer to the vanity and the arrogance of men. He admits, "all men are liars" (Psalm 116:11). It is in distress that we come to learn that God is good. It is in distress that we learn not to rely upon human systems alone but rather to rely upon God—not to trust the arrogance and vanity of mankind. It is in distress that we come to realize that God is good in life and in death.

Let's jump ahead to verse 15. Here the psalmist records what, for me, was a strange verse at first. He says, "precious in the sight of the Lord is the death of his saints." Perhaps you've looked at that text and wondered what it means. Perhaps you also found it strange if you look back at verse 3, where he talks about going through great troubles and has a near death experience. He says, "the cords of death entangled me. Anguish of the grace came upon me. I was overcome by trouble and sorrow. Then I called upon the name of the Lord, Oh Lord save me," (from death). After being delivered and having reflection, he had a different insight. In verse 15, he says, "precious in the sight of the Lord is the death of his saints." What does this mean? It means that when you have a real faith experience with God and you know that God has saved you, you develop a relationship with God out of trust. You know that whether in life or in death you are the Lord's.

Psychologists tell us that death is at the core of what is called the "fundamental anxiety." The fear of death is really one of non-being. When you come to know the goodness of God, you come to understand that death does not have the last word and you begin to lose your fear. You are no longer anxious about death.

As one who has been down to the banks of the Jordan and felt the proverbial spraying mist upon my brow, I can resonate with the words of the psalmist. I know what it is to have a near death experience. On November 23, 1994, at two o'clock in the morning, the surgeons at the Medical College of Virginia sewed up my abdomen and then held it together with staples. I had undergone twelve hours of surgery to replace a liver that had ceased to function. It was a victorious step in what had been a very trying ordeal. Bear with me while I share just a little bit with you.

In July 1994, I got sick, so sick that I couldn't even stand and walk fifteen feet without assistance. I lost all of my muscle tone and flesh in my upper body. I looked from my face down to the top of my abdomen like someone in the last stages of terminal cancer. My stomach was distended; my lower limbs had become so swollen with fluid that the very nerve endings were stretching and my skin looked like it might pop. Just to touch me was extremely painful. When I had to go to the hospital, it would take twenty minutes for me to get my socks on—even the special socks they had prescribed for me. When I went out I had to be pushed in a wheelchair. I remember sitting at the table even though all of my appetite was gone. Everything tasted bitter to me. As I felt my strength leaving, I could remember crying in frustration, "Why was this happening to me?"

There were some saints on the corner of Thirty-first and O Streets in Richmond, Virginia (the Thirty-first Street Baptist Church), who began to pray when they learned of my condition. Other people from all over the nation began to pray. I have at home a large basket full of cards; most of them came from Thirty-first Street Baptist Church members, but some came from all over the country: persons sending me messages of encouragement and support letting me know that they were praying for me. Persons who would travel to other churches would tell me "I went to church in such and such a place, and when they had the altar call, they called your name." They prayed for me. Our choir sang the song, "Somebody Prayed for Me."

Strange as it may seem, I got better. I got strong enough to walk, albeit with a cane. I found some clothes, some old suits, and put them together. I bought some shoes three sizes too large (that's all I could get on my feet). I told myself, "I'm going to church." One Sunday morning, when they had been merely hearing from me by letter and expecting to hear from me by telephone, I walked in on them. The church members began to cry as they stood and applauded. I thought they were applauding the fact that I had made so much progress, that I was doing so well, and that I could actually walk in there. I later learned from one of my young deacons that they were crying because I looked so bad. The interesting thing is they didn't see how bad I really had been looking. I was looking good by the time they saw me. But they kept on praying for me.

They prayed for me everyday for weeks. Then God began to do an amazing thing right before their eyes. God began to bring me back. They began to claim it all over the city: "God is healing our pastor." Some of them were praying that God would heal me without the benefit of surgery, but I knew that God has more than one means of affecting His will. I had prayed, "Lord, whatever your will, whatever you decide I'll submit to it." They had given me a beeper to wear when I was placed on the list to receive a liver transplant. I was the first on the list to receive an organ transplant when one became available. They said, "whenever that beeper goes off, you contact us right away and then make it to the hospital as fast as you can."

When they had done their initial work-up on me, they warned me of a very ominous development. They told me that the liver had malfunctioned so badly that my clotting factor had become seriously compromised. The surgeon, when he began to counsel me in pre-surgery conference, showed me this dark side of the mountain. He said to me, "we can do everything right, and you'll still bleed to death because your clotting factor is so seriously compromised." In fact, he assured me I would probably have to go back into surgery once or twice more just to stop the bleeding that was likely to continue even after I had undergone the transplant. I never shared that with those close to me; I kept that to myself.

So, the beeper stood for not only the call to hope, but also the possibility of being called home to be with the Lord. I had no way of knowing when that beeper went off and whether or not I was being called to my death. Survival from the surgery had not been guaranteed for me. I did not know what God had in mind. I was praying, "Lord, your will be done." Other folks were praying, "Lord heal him." Then one day, because I was doing so well, I asked the liver specialists on my weekly visit to tell me what my numbers were at that point in time. They can take your blood and tell so many things about what's going on inside you. I said, "What are my numbers?" He said, "Well, your bilirubin has improved dramatically, and that's why you're feeling so good." Then he went down and read off a number of things. Eventually, I asked to know my clotting factor results. He gasped, as if someone had hit him in the stomach, as he said, "Why, that's back to normal." I knew then that God had something more for me to do and that I would not die in surgery.

I got so confident that I quit wearing the beeper. I left it home. A couple of weeks later, I was walking through the house one evening and heard the news report that Mr. Crosby of the rock group, Crosby, Stills, and Nash, had received a liver transplant, and there was some controversy over the fact that he had not been on the waiting list very long before he got his liver. They were saying it was probably because of his celebrity status. As I heard it, naturally being on the list for a liver transplant, it caught my attention. But I kept on moving. Then at 11:00 P.M. as I was lying in bed, they re-aired the story. This time they went into greater detail about all of the hundreds of people who die each year because there are no organs available for transplantation. It was as though I heard a voice say to me, "See, so when you get that phone call, don't get cute, don't take it for granted, it's going to be a gift from God." I never closed my eyes all that night. At 4:30 A.M. when the phone rang, I knew who was calling. It was the transplant coordinator. She said, "Dr. Rollins, we've got you a liver." I said, "You know, I'm doing so well, don't you want to pass by me and give it to someone else and catch me another time?" She laughed and said, "Dr. Rollins it doesn't work that way." I said, "If I pass it up, does that mean I'll never get it?" She said, "That's right." I heard that voice say, "Didn't I tell you not to be cute?" So I said, "I'll be in." I had said to the Thirty-first Street congregation that "If God chose to heal me without the benefit of surgery, he could do it. But if God chose surgery as the means by which he would affect his cure, I would submit to whatever God chose." These words came echoing back in my memory.

When I walked in I met some residents and interns that I hadn't seen before; I overheard them say among themselves, "He doesn't look like somebody who's dying of liver failure." They took nineteen vials of blood for their final test before I was to go into surgery. I'll never forget the young lady who took my blood. She asked, "Did they sedate you?" I said, "No, nobody sedated me." She said, "I've never seen anyone go into surgery as calm as you are." I can tell you what my sedative was: I knew that the moment I got that phone call or that beep, and made just one or two phone calls, that a chain reaction would go into place, and the doors of Thirty-first Street Baptist church would open, and saints would gather, and they'd pray me through the surgery. I already knew that. That was my sedative. Then, they took me down and operated on me. For twelve hours, the surgeons did what they are supposed to do. While they were doing what they could do, God was doing what God does. At two o'clock in the morning, they sewed me up. I slept all the next day. The following day, I awoke with tubes all in me unable to talk. I got a pad and started writing notes. When they took the tubes out, I started talking. The next day, they took me out of intensive care, and the following day I walked.

On the fourth day, I sat beside my hospital bed and by telephone patch hookup (it was Sunday morning) I spoke for almost twenty minutes to the saints of Thirty-first Street Baptist Church. I told them that I could look out of my window and see the steeple of the church. "I just want you to know that God is good, and God hears and answers prayer." Eight days later, I walked out of that hospital on my own strength. Eleven days later, I mounted the pulpit of Thirty-first Street Baptist Church. I told them, "To God be the glory, great things he hath done." Then my good friend, Dr. Ben Robertson, prevailed upon me to come on over to Cedar Street. I sat there through his service, then I spoke to his congregation. Because it was on television, many thousands in the Richmond metropolitan area saw it. It was at this time that I launched what had come to be recognized as my new mission, that is, the educational promotion of organ donation and transplantation in the African-American community. Our people, for too many superstitious and erroneous reasons, fail to donate their organs when they die. I believe that God has given us the marvelous opportunity to keep giving the gift of life even as we leave this life.

I pray that all of us would sign our donor cards and inform our loved ones that we want our organs donated when we die. I believe that the God who gave the knowledge to those in the medical profession to perform this surgery has extended my life and ministry through this program. God hears and answers prayer. There is value in distress. God is good in life and in death.

The third and final point is that God's goodness deserves our love, and love seeks a way to repay. Listen to what the psalmist says, beginning at verse 12:

> How can I repay the Lord for all his goodness to me?
> I will lift up the cup of salvation and call on the name of the Lord. I will fulfill my vows to the Lord in the presence of all his people. Precious in the sight of the Lord is the death of his saints. O Lord, truly I am your servant; I am your servant, the son of your maidservant; you have freed me from my chains.
> I will sacrifice a thank offering to you and call on the name of the Lord. I will fulfill my vows to the Lord in the presence of all his people, in the courts of the house of the Lord—in your midst, O Jerusalem.
> Praise the Lord.
>
> —Psalm 116:12–19 NIV

The psalmist begins to reflect "How can I repay?" Love always wants to repay. Love doesn't take anything for granted. Then he declares, "God has been so good to me I'm going to serve Him all the days of my life." Likewise, God has been good to me and "I'm going to pay my vows." I'm just not going to do it privately; I'm going to do it publicly "before all the people."

I don't know about anybody else, but I've got to tell, wherever I go, what the Lord has done for me. Not only did He "heal my body and tell me to run on," He also saved my soul, cleansed me, and made me whole. That took a miracle of love and grace. I declare: the Lord Has Been Good to Me. . . .

—Darrel Rollins

Pastor, Thirty-first Missionary Baptist Church, Richmond, Virginia
Dean of the School of Religion, Shaw University